SARAH ORNE JEWETT

MODERN LITERATURE SERIES
GENERAL EDITOR: Philip Winsor

In the same series:

(continued on last page of book)

SARAH
ORNE JEWETT

Josephine Donovan

FREDERICK UNGAR PUBLISHING CO.
NEW YORK

To Josephine Devigne Donovan
my mother
and William Nelson Donovan
my father

Library of Congress Cataloging in Publication Data

Donovan, Josephine, 1941–
  Sarah Orne Jewett

  Bibliography: p.
  Includes index.
  1. Jewett, Sarah Orne, 1849–1909—Criticism
    and interpretation.

PS2133.D6   813′.4   80-5334
ISBN 0-8044-2137-4

Contents

Acknowledgements

I would like to thank the following people who have in one way or another helped make this book possible: Elizabeth Goodwin, Jeanne Aspinwall, Anne Barrett, Barbara White, Lina Mainiero and Philip Winsor.

Chronology

1877   *Deephaven*, first book-length collection of sketches, published by Osgood and Company.

Late 1870s   Lifelong relationship with Annie Adams Fields begins.

20 September 1878   Father, Theodore Herman Jewett, dies.

1878   *Play Days*, a book of stories for children, published.

1879   *Old Friends and New* published.

23 April 1881   James T. Fields, Boston publisher and husband of Annie Fields, dies.

1881   *Country By-Ways* published.

1882   First trip to Europe with Annie Fields; visits chiefly England and France, also Belgium, Ireland, Italy, Norway and Switzerland; meets Christina Rossetti, Anne Thackeray Ritchie and Alfred, Lord Tennyson.

1884   *The Mate of the Daylight, and Friends Ashore* published.

                A Country Doctor published.

1885   *A Marsh Island* published.

Fall 1885   First translation of a Jewett work ("A Little Traveler") appears in Paris by Marie Thérèse Blanc; followed by *A Country Doctor* and other stories.

1886   *A White Heron and Other Stories* published.

1888   *The King of Folly Island and Other People* published.

1890   *Betty Leicester* and *Strangers and Wayfarers* published.

                Vacations with Annie Fields in St. Petersburg, Florida.

21 October 1891   Caroline Frances Perry Jewett, her mother, dies.

1892   Second trip to Europe with Annie Fields; meets, among others, Mark Twain; visits

1

Transfiguration through
Friendship: Introduction
and Biographical Sketch

Women had been successful authors in the United
States since the earliest years of the republic.
Susanna Rowson's *Charlotte Temple,* a sensational
best seller, was first published in Philadelphia in
1794. Women writers continued to dominate
American popular fiction throughout the
nineteenth century. From 1820 to 1870 "women's
fiction" was an identifiable genre, one that focused
on the trials and tribulations of a noble heroine
"winning her own way in the world."[1]

Women writers produced prodigiously upon
this sentimental theme, and they were prodigiously
successful. In the decade of the 1850s all the works
of Hawthorne, Melville, Thoreau and Whitman put
together were outsold by any one of a number of the
popular women's novels of the period.[2] The
women's fiction was, however, put down by the male
authors. Nathaniel Hawthorne, perhaps jealous of
their commercial success, referred to them as a
"damned mob of scribbling women," and complained that their work was corrupting the literary
marketplace.

By the late 1850s, and especially after the advent of the *Atlantic Monthly* in 1857, some women
writers began to put forth a new kind of fiction,
which was more realistic and dealt with common-

1

place subjects in specific locales, often with humor. The pioneers of this movement, which came to be known as the "local color" school, were Rose Terry (later Cooke) (1827–1892) and Harriet Beecher Stowe (1811–1896). Both published stories in the first issue of the *Atlantic Monthly* (1857): "Sally Parson's Duty" and "The Mourning Veil," respectively. Soon after, the *Atlantic* published Rebecca Harding Davis's grimly realistic "Life in the Iron Mills" (1861), a far cry from sentimental romance.

In the same year, Rose Terry provided a brief announcement of the new genre in her preface to "Miss Lucinda," a tale about a spinster.

Forgive me . . . patient reader, if I offer to you no tragedy in high life, no sentimental history of fashion and wealth, but only a little story about *a woman who could not be a heroine.* [3]

Terry's statement expressed a conscious rejection of the earlier tradition of women's literature with its romantic "heroines" and "sentimental histories." It signaled the beginning of a new movement in American literature, the genius of which was to bloom in the masterworks of Sarah Orne Jewett.

* * *

Theodora Sarah Orne Jewett was born on 3 September 1849 in South Berwick, a town on the southern border of Maine, about ten miles up the Piscataqua River from the Atlantic Ocean. The stories and novels that were to make her famous are set in the southern tier of Maine, especially the seacoast area, where she lived most of her life. Her literary reputation rests upon more than 170 works of fiction, most of which depict the lives of the ordinary people of nineteenth-century rural Maine. Her life began in the age of horse-drawn carriages and sailing ships and ended in the early twentieth century, the era of the automobile and the telephone, inventions she herself enjoyed using.

Sarah was born into an established and wealthy family. Her grandfather, Captain Theodore Furber Jewett (1787–1860), had prospered as a shipowner and merchant in the West Indies trade in the early part of the century and had left the family financially independent. For Sarah Orne Jewett, as she herself acknowledged, writing was never to be "a bread and butter affair."

The house in which she was born, a distinguished Georgian structure, had been purchased by Captain Jewett for the family ten years before Sarah's birth. It still stands in the center of South Berwick, much as it was in Sarah's day, well cared for by the Society for the Preservation of New England Antiquities. It is open to the public in summers.

Sarah's early years were spent in a preindustrial maritime society. She often heard tales told by sailors of adventures at sea. Her father, Theodore Herman Jewett (1815-1878), was a locally well respected country physician. Her mother, Caroline Frances Perry (1820–1891), was descended from the Perry and Gilman families of Exeter, New Hampshire. Through the Gilmans, she was a distant descendent of Anne Bradstreet. Sarah had two sisters, one older, Mary Rice (1847–1930), and one younger, Caroline (1855–1897).

The young Sarah Jewett was educated at Miss Raynes's School and at Berwick Academy in South Berwick, from which she graduated in 1866. By her own admission, she was a somewhat listless student. She later remarked that her real education had come from her father, whom she often accompanied on house calls. He brought to her his extensive knowledge of nature and of literature, urging her to indulge in the classic authors in his library, such as Cervantes, Fielding, Sterne, Smollett, and Walton. Sarah's mother and grandmother, however, introduced her to works by Jane Austen, George Eliot and Mrs. Margaret Oliphant (1828–1897), a Scottish novelist whose works focused on provincial English society in the nineteenth century. Sarah mentions reading only Oliphant's *Miss Marjoribanks* in her 1869 diary, but the Jewett library held fifteen of her works.[4] Jewett retained her admiration for Jane Austen throughout her life and reread *Persuasion* with great enjoyment in her later years. George Eliot, on the other hand, was never a favorite, though Jewett's library included all Eliot's major works.

It is probably through the influence of this early reading that Sarah developed a sense of what serious, quality literature was. As a young writer, she seems to have identified herself more with the classic European tradition than with any native authors. It was only later, when exposed to the critical guidance of editors like William Dean Howells that she linked up with the indigenous local color school and its predominantly female authors.

One cannot overestimate the influence of her father in the formulation of Sarah Orne Jewett's literary standards. Over and over in letters she wrote as an adult to younger writers she repeats pieces of advice gleaned from him. Already in her diary of 1871 she had penciled on the inside cover what would later become an important tenet of her literary credo:

Father said this one day "A story should be managed so that it should *suggest* interesting things to the *reader* instead of the author's doing all the thinking for him, and setting it before him in black and white. The best compliment is for the reader to say 'Why didn't he put in "this" or "that." ' "[5]

The idea promoted here is not too far removed from the aesthetic theory of the Impressionist painters or the Symbolist poets—that the artist's job is to create the suggestion, the impression of a scene; the viewer's is to fill it in. But unlike the Impressionists and Symbolists, Jewett insisted that the artist must attend to life in "its everyday aspects." "My dear father used to say to me very often, 'Tell things *just as they are!*' and used to show me what he meant in [Sterne's satiric novel] *A Sentimental Journey!*"

These pieces of parental advice she found summarized in two mottoes from Flaubert, which she later pinned onto the back of her secretary: "Écrire la vie ordinaire comme on écrit l'histoire," and "Ce n'est pas de faire rire, ni de faire pleurer, ni de vous mettre à fureur, mais d'agir à la façon de la nature, c'est à dire de faire rêver." To an extent these statements sum up what Jewett tried to do in her own work: to dignify ordinary life by elevating it to the level of history, and to suggest, to figure forth a dimension of higher significance in the contingent order.

We are fortunate to have several diaries that young Jewett kept sporadically in her late teens and early twenties. These tell us much about her personality, her reading tastes, and her daily life, which was typically that of a well-born young "lady" of the period.

In her 1869 diary, the first third of which was written while she was in Cincinnati visiting relatives, we find that her days were spent in sewing, in drawing lessons, and in reading voraciously. Every Sunday in its entirety was spent in church, but the young Sarah was not a natural churchgoer. Her mind wandered, she made faces across the aisle at friends, and she complained of the boredom and stupidity of certain sermons. The diaries are filled, however,

with self-remonstrances: not to be "cross" or to say
"wicked" things, to try to think more often of God.[6]
One senses that like Jo in *Little Women,* a comparison
she herself once made, young Sarah had trouble
toeing the mark.

While Sarah's early efforts at religion seem
more rhetorical than real, there were other aspects
of her life that she took quite seriously. One, not
surprising perhaps in retrospect, was the strong
sense she had of her own future. The other was a
network of friends that provided her with primary
emotional connections, or with what today we might
call a "support group."

That Sarah early had a peculiar sense of her
own destiny may be seen in a diary entry written
when she was eighteen years old. In it she muses,

I think it would be funny if a hundred years from now
some girl like me should find this diary somewhere and
wonder about me.[7]

A similar idea is suggested in a comment made in
1872 in which she half-humorously intimated that
her letters may someday be "preserved in a volume."
And by 1873 she could announce to her first editor,
Horace Scudder, "I am getting quite ambitious and
really feel that writing is my work." Scudder was
editor of the *Riverside Magazine for Young Folks* from
1867 to 1870 and in that capacity he accepted two of
Jewett's earliest stories, "The Shipwrecked Buttons"
and "The Girl With the Cannon Dresses" (both in
1870). He became editor-in-chief of the *Atlantic
Monthly* in 1890.

Equally important to the young woman's development as an artist, however, were the emotional
ties she had with several friends, all of them young
women her own age. In many cases these reached
the level of intense crushes. One of these relation-

ships, that with Kate Birckhead of Newport, Rhode Island, is especially significant because it seems likely that Kate Birckhead was fictionalized as the protagonist of Jewett's first major collection, *Deephaven.*

Sarah noted in a diary entry in 1872 that she would do anything to demonstrate the depth of her feelings for Kate.[8] It appears that this desire became an important motivation in the development of the *Deephaven* sketches. The first of these were published in the September 1873 issue of the *Atlantic Monthly,* less than a year after the diary notation. The sketches, later entitled "Kate Lancaster's Plan" and "The Brandon House and the Lighthouse," were originally published in the *Atlantic* under the title "The Shore House." *Deephaven* is structured upon a fictional relationship between two young women similar to the real bond between Sarah and Kate Birckhead described in the diary.

The 1869 diary is especially useful, because it gives us an idea of young Jewett's early reading tastes. It was a significant year in her life, as it was probably during this period that she first began to consider a writing career seriously. She had already published one story, "Jenny Garrow's Lovers," under the pseudonym A. C. Eliot in the 18 January 1868 issue of *The Flag of Our Union,* a Boston weekly. And during the year she was to publish her first story in the *Atlantic Monthly,* "Mr. Bruce."

During the year Sarah read a wide variety of materials: serious essays by Macauley, Charles Lamb and John Stuart Mill; George Sand's *Fanchon;* Dickens's *Great Expectations* and *Oliver Twist;* Elizabeth Barrett Browning's *Aurora Leigh;* Goethe's *Wilhelm Meister,* Elizabeth Stuart Phelps's *The Gates Ajar,* and Louisa May Alcott's *Little Women* (for the second time), to name but a few. One of her favorite

books was Ouïda's *Under Two Flags.* She also read
some sentimental works, such as Adeline Dutton
Train Whitney's *Patience Strong's Outing,* which she
found "rather spoony."[9]

Jewett later singled out Harriet Beecher Stowe's
novel, *The Pearl of Orr's Island* (1862), as the most
influential work she read as a youth. Stowe's novel
was cluttered with the trappings of sentimental romance, such as abandoned orphans miraculously
washed up on beaches and women who stereotypically exemplified what has been called the "cult of
true womanhood."[10] Nevertheless, it portrayed certain characters realistically and in a real setting,
Orr's Island, off the coast of Maine. Stowe also used
local dialect, which was soon to become the hallmark
of the local color school. Jewett recognized the
characters, the dialect and the setting; this was a
world she knew well. Stowe's book made her realize
that she too could build fiction from materials taken
from the Maine countryside she loved so well.

George Sand's *Légendes Rustiques* may have been
another early influence. Jewett remained enam-
ored of George Sand throughout her life. A por-
trait of the great French writer hung over the mantle
of Jewett's South Berwick home, and she reportedly
spent one summer learning French so that she could
read Sand in the original.

Other possible influences have been suggested
because of their similarity to Jewett's work. These
include Theocritus's *Idyls,* Elizabeth Gaskell's
Cranford, Sir Walter Scott's Waverley novels, and the
works of Flaubert, Mary Russell Mitford, and
Dorothy Wordsworth. Tolstoy and Turgenev might
be added to the list, as Jewett herself drew compari-
sons between certain of their works and hers, and
Thackeray remained perhaps her favorite author.

About Flaubert, whom one might wish to see as
Jewett's master, she was most enthusiastic. ("It is

quite wonderful how great a book Flaubert makes of *Madame Bovary*.") However, she found Emma Bovary exasperating for her failure to recognize "what there was in that dull little village! She is such a lesson to country dwellers who drift out of relation to their surroundings, not only social but the very companionships of nature, unknown to them." This statement shows clearly Jewett's own belief in the worth and interest of provincial life.

Throughout the year 1869 Sarah also read diligently at back issues of some of the major periodicals of her day, *Harper's Weekly, Harper's Magazine,* the *Atlantic Monthly* and *North American Review*. She mentions reading aloud to her grandmother a favorite story, Elizabeth Stuart Phelps's "Kentucky's Ghost" from the November 1868 *Atlantic*.[11]

The *Atlantic Monthly* was by this time under the editorship of James T. Fields (1817–1881), with William Dean Howells (1837–1920) acting as his associate. Howells would take over as editor-in-chief in 1871. In perusing the *Atlantic*s of the 1860s, Sarah Orne Jewett would have found many works by women authors, especially during and immediately after the Civil War. Regular contributors included Rose Terry (later Cooke), Louisa May Alcott, Gail Hamilton, Caroline Chesebro, Harriet E. Prescott (later Spofford), Rebecca Harding Davis, Elizabeth Stuart Phelps (later Ward), and Harriet Beecher Stowe. Many of these, especially Cooke, Spofford and Stowe, later became important members of Jewett's own literary circle.

The young author might also have read theoretical works in the pages of the *Atlantic,* articles by T. W. Higginson such as "Literature As an Art" in 1867 or "Americanism in Literature" in 1870, in which he picked up Emerson's earlier call for a native American literature, one that dealt with local people and issues, encouraging the growth of the "local color" movement. Or, earlier in the decade, she might have taken note of T. W. Higginson's attack on the sentimental in literature in his "A Letter to the Young Contributor" (1862).

But it was undoubtedly William Dean Howells in his capacity as editor at the *Atlantic* who had the most immediate influence on Jewett in her formative years as a writer from the late 1860s through the early 1880s. Howells's own literary standards had pretty well crystalized by this time. Unlike the earlier giants of the so-called American Renaissance in literature, Melville, Hawthorne and Poe, Howells's world view was characteristically American: optimistic, positivistic, neoclassical in spirit.

In his study of Howells, Everett Carter suggests that the era of American literature over which Howells presided was like any neoclassical period an "age of comedy." By this he did not mean comedy in the sense of farce or riotous laughter, but comedy in the sense of an affirmative view of the world, which is seen as a cohesive, secure structure. "The comic writer believes in the significance of the social organism of which he is a part."[12]

To some extent Jewett shared in Howells's neoclassical spirit and comic vision. Unlike writers of the twentieth century for whom things had "fallen apart" and whose vision was often one of anarchy and alienation, Jewett and Howells belonged to and affirmed a society in which the center still held and the community still functioned as a viable social unit, however tenuously.

Like Higginson, Howells was concerned that writers begin to deal with the reality of their American environment, and he rejected sentimentalism in literature because of its fraudulence. He favored works that were autobiographical, that hovered on the edge of nonfiction. From his earliest days at the

Atlantic "he encouraged writers to give him stories about people and places they knew, without worrying about plot or incident."

When books came across his reviewing desk which contained truthful characterizations in clearly observed settings, he cheered for them . . . ; when the pieces he received were lacking in these elements, he would ask the contributor to get more sense of "locality" into his stories and articles.[13]

Sarah Orne Jewett first corresponded with Howells in 1869 when she submitted "Mr. Bruce" to the *Atlantic*. As editorial comments were done anonymously, Sarah knew him only as "the Editor with the fine handwriting" and so addressed one of her early letters to him. Howells accepted her story after she agreed to make some slight revisions.

Soon after this, Jewett submitted a sketch that was even more to his taste. "The Shore House" realistically described authentic Maine figures in their own setting, had a minimum of plot, and was close to being autobiographical. Howells was enthusiastic in his praise of this new direction in Jewett's writing and encouraged her eventually to put the series of sketches of the Maine coast together as *Deephaven* in 1877.

While Jewett may have learned much from Howells and shared many of his literary and philosophical attitudes, it would be a mistake to consider the controlling vision in her mature work as comic. To be sure she wrote many stories that are essentially humorous, such as her most anthologized piece, "The Dulham Ladies" (1886). Yet Sarah Orne Jewett's ultimate vision was elegaic. In her most important fiction, she mourned the passing of a world in which nature was still a sanctuary, in which community was still a possibility, and in which women of

strength were the prime sustainers of the communal
experience. These themes are given their fullest expression in the work that is considered to be her
masterpiece, *The Country of the Pointed Firs* (1896).

From her earliest letters we find evidence of
Jewett's strong resistance to the forces of indus-
trialism and "progress." It was as if she instinctively
knew that the mass production and mass communi-
cation systems of the twentieth century would
threaten to destroy forever the precious particulars
of the rural landscape. After the Civil War New
England converted from a region whose primary
economy revolved around the sea to one which de-
pended on industry, mills, railroads, and cheap
human labor. After the war a mill was built only a
mile from Sarah's own house in South Berwick. The
ultimate result of such industrial expansion was of
course the ruin of the natural environment.

In an early sketch Sarah lamented the destruction of a nearby forest:

The woods I loved best had all been cut down the winter
before. I had played under the great pines when I was a
child, and I had spent many a long afternoon under them
since. There never will be such trees for me any more in
the world. I know where the flowers grew under them,
and where the ferns were greenest, and it was as much
home to me as my own house.[14]

"Berwick," she remarked in 1877, "is growing and
flourishing in a way that breaks my heart." And
many years later when she heard of a plan to sub-
divide the beautiful Piscataqua riverbank, she cried
out that such developments gave her "a hunted feeling like the last wild thing that is left in the fields."

Jewett once remarked that when she first began
submitting material for publication, she had no
"literary friends 'at court.' " Yet it was not long after
her initial successes that she moved into the center of

Boston literary society and become fast friends with its reigning figures, James T. and Annie Adams Fields (1834–1915).

James was probably the most important editor and publisher of his day. Annie served as an unofficial assistant editor for him, handling manuscripts by women especially. It is known that he deferred often to her judgment; it seems likely, for example, that it was her decision that his firm, Ticknor & Fields, publish Elizabeth Stuart Phelps's *The Gates Ajar* in 1868. It became an all-time bestseller. Annie Fields made the Fieldses' home at 148 Charles Street in Boston a celebrated literary salon.

After James's death in 1881, Sarah's already close relationship with Annie intensified. This became the most important relationship of Jewett's adult life. It ended only with Sarah's death in 1909. The lifestyle that the two evolved was that Sarah would spend approximately half the year with Annie, either in Boston or at the Fieldses' ocean-front cottage in Manchester-by-the-Sea, Massachusetts. The rest of the time she spent with her family in South Berwick, where Annie would visit occasionally. Apparently Sarah wrote in all of these places.

They formed what used to be called a "Boston marriage": a life-long monogamous partnership between two women. This was a fairly common social unit in the nineteenth century.[15] By the 1890s Sarah and Annie were treated as a couple by correspondents and friends. Richard Cary, in reviewing the nearly three hundred letters written to Sarah Orne Jewett that are now in the Colby College collection, commented that

the ineludible verity met at almost every turn of the page in this accumulation is the soundness and constancy of the connection between Miss Jewett and Mrs. Fields. . . .

Their unswerving affection for each other is exposed in
reflex image here. Almost every letter to one . . . em-
bodies a notation about the other.[16]

Jewett's passionate devotion to Annie Fields
may also be seen in a series of letters she wrote near
the beginning of their relationship and in a number
of unpublished love poems that were clearly written
to Annie Fields. The letters and the poetry are in the
Houghton Library at Harvard University. Whether
or not one is to call this a lesbian relationship depends upon one's definition of the term. If it is
narrowly defined as a purely physical attraction, it
would not seem to apply. If defined as an intense
love relationship between women, it would.[17]

Mark Anthony DeWolfe Howe, a literary historian, urged Annie Fields to delete intimate material from her 1911 edition of Jewett's letters, which
she did. Such censorship has not served critics and
readers well, for it has allowed to go unchecked the
image of Jewett as a passionless spinster. The litany
of illustrious critics who have fallen into the trap of
interpreting her works in terms of this erroneous
stereotype is long indeed. It includes Paul Elmer
More, Vernon L. Parrington, Granville Hicks, and
Van Wyck Brooks.

The real Jewett was quite removed from this
false image. As one observer noted, in all our pictures of her, "there is a full-lipped, clear-browed,
unembarrassed handsomeness which speaks of the
Cavalier spirit at its best."[18] Sarah was described as
being beautiful by many who knew her. She had
large brown eyes, a wide forehead, and dark hair.
She was moderately tall. While never in very good
health (she suffered from regular attacks of
rheumatism) she was a vigorous horsewoman who
occasionally traveled alone on extended trips, such

as the thirty-mile trek from South Berwick to Amesbury, Massachusetts, to the home of poet John Greenleaf Whittier. She was a lover of animals, had several dogs and cats, and was on the board of the Maine SPCA.

As an adult Jewett lived at the center of a vital and successful artistic community composed primarily of women writers and artists. This network provided emotional support as well as critical encouragement for its members. In her later years Jewett recognized how important these friends had been to her, when she commented that there was "something transfiguring in the best of friendship." It gives us "shining hours" that sustain us when we descend "from the mountain . . . into the fret of everyday life." Such moments of transcendence validate our daily tasks and give us the courage to persevere. Much of Jewett's fiction, like all great literature, deals with moments in which characters "move beyond" the fallen, limited state of their everyday world. Jewett's model for such transcendence was the community of women she was a part of, and particularly her relationship with Annie Adams Fields. Not surprisingly, in much of her writing female friendships provide the transcending leap.

Included in her network were Celia Thaxter (1835–1894), a New Hampshire poet; Louise Imogen Guiney (1861–1920), poet and essayist; Sarah Wyman Whitman (1842–1904), an artist to whom Jewett dedicated her *Strangers and Wayfarers* (1890); Sara Norton (1864–1922), a cellist and daughter of Charles Eliot Norton, president of Harvard; Marie Thérèse Blanc (1840–1907), who translated Jewett's work into French and was herself the author of several articles and works of fiction; and Alice Greenwood Howe (1835–1924), one of the founders of the

Boston Symphony Orchestra, to whom Jewett dedicated *The Country of the Pointed Firs*. Jewett was also a close friend of Quaker poet Whittier (1807–1892) and author and editor Thomas Bailey Aldrich (1836–1907). With the exception of Madame Blanc, all of these people lived in or near Boston.

In addition, Jewett maintained an extensive correspondence. Important letter collections remain between her and Louisa Loring Dresel (1864–1958); Violet Paget, alias Vernon Lee, (1850–1935); Mary Rice Jewett, her sister; Lilian Munger; and Anna Laurens Dawes.[19]

She also knew or corresponded with Elizabeth Stuart Phelps Ward (1844–1911); Harriet Beecher Stowe (1811–1896); Mary E. Wilkins Freeman (1852–1930); Alice French, alias Octave Thanet, (1850–1934); Mary E. Noailles Murfree, alias George Craddock, (1850–1922); Alice Brown (1857–1948); Rose Terry Cooke, (1827–1892); Harriet Prescott Spofford (1835–1921); Helen Hunt Jackson (1830–1885); Sarah Chauncey Woolsey, alias Susan Coolidge, (1835–1905); Louise Chandler Moulton (1835–1908); Laura Richards (1850–1943); Julia Ward Howe (1819–1910); May Sinclair (1865–1946); and Willa Cather (1876–1947). With the exception of May Sinclair, who was British, this listing includes most of the important American women authors of her day.

Annie Fields and Sarah Orne Jewett took four trips to Europe, in 1882, 1892, 1898 and 1900. During these voyages they met some of the most celebrated literary figures of the time, including Alfred, Lord Tennyson, Henry James, Mark Twain, Anne Thackeray Ritchie, Rudyard Kipling, and Christina Rossetti. Matthew Arnold, Charles Dickens and Oliver Wendell Holmes, Jr. had been among the regular visitors to 148 Charles Street. While in

Europe, Sarah made special pilgrimages to the homes of Madame de Sévigné in Grignan, France, and the Brontë sisters, in Haworth, England.

Jewett was brought up a Congregationalist and was confirmed an Episcopalian. But like many nineteenth-century women, she found certain aspects of the establishment religions unappealing, especially any remnants of Calvinism with its harsh doctrine of damnation. In several of her works she rejects this fire-and-brimstone, patriarchal religion in favor of a more compassionate, humanistic creed.

But from an early age her true religious interests inclined toward an unorthodox, spiritualistic faith. In part this was due to the encouragement of an early mentor, Theophilus Parsons, a Harvard law professor who was a Swedenborgian. Emmanuel Swedenborg (1688–1772) had promoted a mystical theology that emphasized an arcane correspondence between the material world and the spiritual, between the microcosm and the macrocosm, between body and soul. He also asserted the redemptive powers of human and divine love. His doctrines became quite popular in the nineteenth century, especially among the Symbolist poets, but even a "realist" like William Dean Howells had been brought up on Swedenborgianism. Under Parsons's influence, Jewett had read Swedenborg's work and once said that she found "a sense of it under everything else."

From other comments she made in letters to Annie Fields, we can determine that it was the body-soul problem that most concerned her. Death, she maintained, must be a moment of waking, analogous to birth. Perhaps in the next life we will celebrate our death day as we do our birthday in this life. Concerning literature, she lamented the imperfect shape one's thoughts ended up taking and wondered whether in another life the poet's thoughts might bloom untended, without material troubles such as editing, "covers, leaves and publishing."

She believed in what we now call extrasensory perception, and in 1905 compared it to the newly developed wireless telegraph. Perhaps her most intriguing meditations on spiritual reality came at the death of Celia Thaxter in 1894. She stated in a letter to Annie Fields that she seemed to be able to see Celia's face, and she began to wonder "where imagination stops and consciousness of the unseen begins, who can settle that even to one's self?"

In 1902 Jewett suffered serious spinal injuries and a concussion after being thrown from a carriage. In the spring of 1909 she had a stroke and on 24 June 1909 died in her home at South Berwick as she had wished, "leaving the lilac bushes still green, and all the chairs in their places."

Shortly afterwards, Annie Fields wrote,

She used to say we must learn not to be so dependent upon bodily presence . . . it is indeed true that having laid aside her beautiful body she now seems very near to me in many loving ways which are all her own and greatly comforted & companioned by her.[20]

2

The Artist as a Young Woman:
From *Play Days* to *Deephaven* and *Old Friends and New*

On 13 July 1872, Sarah Orne Jewett took note in her diary of a criticism by Charles Lamb that a book could be too "preachy" and full of literal scripture, but that no book could have "too much of silent scripture" in it. She resolved not to write "parsonish" stories herself, but to retain a level of moral meaning, of "silent scripture," in her work.[1]

During her first decade of publishing—up to about 1880—Jewett put forth nearly forty stories, most of which were collected into three books: *Deephaven* (1877), *Play Days* (1878) and *Old Friends and New* (1879). In many of these stories the scriptural element is not so silent as one might perhaps wish. However, the moral messages that Jewett attempted to convey are themselves an interesting documentation of social attitudes in Victorian America. They reveal some of the tensions that she was experiencing as a writer and as a woman, tensions that she would have to resolve before she could move into a mature sense of her own fictional vision. By the end of the decade she had made significant progress to this end.

Jewett's first published story is quite uncharacteristic of her later work. "Jenny Garrow's Lovers" (*The Flag of Our Union* 18 January 1868, *Uncollected*

Stories 1971) was indeed written by "A. C. Eliot." It is a romantic melodrama set in rural England, a region Jewett only knew from her own reading of romantic novels. The plot concerns two brothers, Will and Dick, who compete in courtship for the heroine, Jenny Garrow. One night Will disappears. Dick is unjustly accused and convicted of Will's murder. He is sent to prison. Jenny in the meantime dies of the plague. Will finally returns five years later to explain that he had left town and gone to sea after Jenny rejected him. Dick is then released, and they both eventually die unmarried.

Perhaps Jewett exhausted her interest in plot in her first story, for there are more dramatic episodes in it—three deaths, a plague, imprisonment, and several broken hearts—than in almost any of her subsequent works. However, we may note that already in this story Jewett's style is tight and spare and surprisingly polished for a novice. And already Jewett has begun experimenting with narrative technique. The story is narrated in the first person by an elderly woman, Margery Blake, who had known Jenny Garrow in her youth; the episodes described had occurred forty years earlier. This was a device Jewett was to use often. Ironically, the narrator apologizes in an opening address to the reader for her lack of narrative skill.

"Mr. Bruce" (*Atlantic Monthly* December 1869, *Old Friends and New* 1879), also by "A. C. Eliot," is quite different. The setting is one its author knew well, the upper-middle-class Boston domestic scene, and its central theme of role playing or masquerading is one that fascinated Jewett throughout the early years of her literary production.

Again we find a self-conscious concern with narrative structure. The opening section of the story is narrated by Aunt Mary, a "maiden lady," to her twenty-year-old niece Elly (probably a Jewett persona), about another maiden lady friend of hers, Miss Margaret Tarrant of Boston. Miss Tarrant, who "possesses the art of telling a story capitally," picks up the narrative line and tells a tale, set twenty to thirty years earlier, about her older sister Kitty and how she met her husband, Mr. Bruce. The central episode is a dinner party where, as a lark, Kitty had volunteered to help out by acting as a servant girl at the table. She even assumed an Irish brogue for the occasion, as most of the Boston working class was in those days Irish. This was all unbeknownst to Mr. Bruce, who later met Kitty in her real role as fashionable Brahmin debutante, much to his surprise and Kitty's amusement.

Like many of Jewett's early stories, this one gives us insights into the lives and attitudes of leisure class adolescent females of the period. Often these seem irritatingly frivolous and naive, yet in her diary writings Jewett shows another side to this coin; she speaks of being "restless and unhappy" and of an "unaccountable melancholy" and "loneliness."[2] Unfortunately, Sarah never dealt directly with these themes in her fiction about adolescents, so that what remains is a rose-colored version of their lives.

Another early story, "The Girl With the Cannon Dresses," (*Riverside Magazine* August 1870, *Uncollected Stories* 1971), the first to be signed "Sarah Jewett," presents another Jewett persona, eighteen-year-old Alice Channing, who is sent "up country" to northern New Hampshire for the summer to recuperate from an illness. An archetypal Jewett pattern emerges when Alice meets Dulcy, a younger version of herself, in the woods.

In this natural setting the two form with the animals a kind of secret society against the adult world. Alice remarks:

When I go back home, I shall wear "grown-up clothes,"
. . . and feel old, and go to school, . . . and while I'm up
here I'll make believe I am just as old as you; we won't tell
any one, for they might think it silly, but we will have the
nicest times in the world.

The tension between the unspoiled, benign world of
nature as opposed to the unpleasant "adult" world
of civilization is one that recurs throughout Jewett's
work. Almost always nature, particularly the woods,
is seen as a haven of escape.

In 1870 Jewett also published "The Shipwrecked Buttons" (*Riverside Magazine* January
1870), the first of fifteen children's stories to be
collected as *Play Days* (1878). Like many of these
stories "The Shipwrecked Buttons" is a fantasy in
which inanimate objects, in this case buttons, come
to life. The story follows the characteristic
narrative-within-a-narrative format.

It opens with Kitty and Jack, sister and brother,
playing sailboat with four buttons who are desig-
nated the Captain, his wife, and two mates. The
children are distracted and run off with the boat still
asail. The story then shifts to the buttons who, after
being shipwrecked, tell their stories.

That Jewett had to a high degree what Keats
called a "negative capability" is very much in evidence in this story. Keats had associated the em-
pathetic ability to get "inside" another creature with
Shakespeare's greatest metaphors. This talent is
seen here in the imaginative button's-eye view of the
world that Jewett creates. The perspective is that of a
very small creature who is a pawn in the hands of its
unaware owners. To some extent Jewett has captured the perspective of a child who could also feel a
pawn of "grown-ups." Or it could be the perspective
of any oppressed group that lacks control over its

life. In this regard Jewett's extraordinary empathy for children and other small creatures may well stem from her own limited situation as a woman in late nineteenth-century America. Several of her later stories, as well as her first novel, *A Country Doctor* (1884), deal explicitly with the discriminations and prejudices that kept women from full participation in worldly ("grown up") affairs. This particular story ends grimly: the buttons are drowned, because their owners forget to reclaim them.

A somewhat similar tale, "The Yellow Kitten" (*The Independent* 6 June 1872), deals with animated spools who avenge themselves on a cat that has pestered them. The story is told by another cat. Spool society is described at length in terms that become a mild satire of human society.

"The Best China Saucer" (*The Independent* 25 July 1872) is one of the most interesting of Jewett's children's stories. This is a moralistic tale whose ostensible message is to "mind your mother." Nelly Willis has been told not to play with Jane, a neighbor child, who is "very naughty": she swears, has bad manners, is dirty, and in the past has incited Nelly to disobedience. Naturally, Nelly ends up playing with Jane only to find that Jane has around her neck a "fly-necklace," a string run through several flies, most of which are still alive and buzzing. This grotesquerie shocks and revolts Nelly, who thus regrets her disobedience. Jane is a curious character who appears to be irretrievably evil. Partly this is a matter of her being of a lower social class, but Jewett specifies that her main problem is that "she would not take the trouble" to be "good and kind and honest and clean."

This is the first of many stories in which an archaic sense of class consciousness is evident. Usually, however, Jewett expresses compassion for the

poor and urges upon the wealthy a sense of obliga-
tion. The story also reflects another of Jewett's basic
moral principles, however: that one can better one's
situation or at least make it tolerable with the right
attitude and a goodly amount of effort. This characteristically American or Emersonian optimism recurs in much of her early writing.

In an unpublished critique of George Eliot's
Middlemarch that she wrote at about this time, Jewett
expressed this position most succinctly.

I have no patience when George Eliot talks of the "meanness of opportunity" so illy matched to Dorothea's
spiritual grandeur! That never fails to make its
opportunity![3]

This exasperation is similar to that which she later
expressed toward Emma Bovary (see chapter 1). By
contrast, most of Jewett's own characters take hold
of the circumstances of their lives and do not suc-
cumb to them. However, Jewett's sense of the
pathos, if not the tragedy, of wasted lives and paltry
circumstances deepened as she grew older. And certainly even in her early stories she expresses a decided ambivalence toward spiritual poverty.

Of the early stories that deal with this theme,
perhaps the most optimistic is "Beyond the Toll-
Gate" (*Sunday Afternoon* March 1878, *Play Days*
1878). Jewett later wrote, rather vaguely, that she
had tried in this story and in two others ("Lady
Ferry" and "The Gray Man") to do something
analogous to what Tolstoy had done in his short
fiction. Presumably this was to present a sense of an
other transcendent reality, with attendant moral
overtones.

With this in mind, one is led to interpret
"Beyond the Toll-Gate" as a moral allegory. It deals
with a young girl, Barbara Snow, who has just moved
to the country with her parents. In her wanderings

near their new house, she discovers a toll-gate which requires a one-cent passage charge. She begins to fantasize about how wonderful it must be beyond the gate. One day she finds a three-cent piece, and her mother grants her permission to use it for the toll. Barbara goes on her adventure and discovers on the other side elderly twin sisters who invite her in and treat her as a special guest. She has a wonderful time and returns home "both rich and happy." It turns out the sisters are old friends of her mother's. The moral of the story is that, while "it costs something to go through," often there is something surprising and delightful on the other side of the gate.

The optimism and security expressed in this story are quite extraordinary for a twentieth-century reader, who expects the child to be injured the minute she steps outdoors. It is interesting to contrast this story with a more contemporary work like James Joyce's *Dubliners,* the early stories of which deal similarly with quests made by youthful protagonists outside their own bailiwicks. In the Joyce stories, the young characters almost always encounter an evil, disillusioning person or event that sends them back home chastened and beaten. By contrast, Jewett's Barbara Snow is rewarded for her venturesomeness; all the people she meets on her journey are benign and helpful.

In a somewhat later but still early story, "A Guest At Home" (*Congregationalist* 29 November 1882, *Uncollected Stories* 1971), Jewett treats the theme of adjusting to limited circumstances in a more autobiographical manner. Annie Hollis, who is in her early twenties, has just returned home to her parents' farm in rural New England after having attended art school in New York.

She had always been a little impatient from her childhood of the bare walls, and the plain, hard life of the farm. . . .

People had said that it was a pity so bright a girl, with such appreciation of the things that can be found in better houses and in the more artistic and cultivated society of a city, should be forced to live in a dull farming town, where there would be so little companionship and sympathy.

Consequently, Annie finds readjustment difficult at first. Eventually, however, she begins to realize that there are many possibilities and opportunities to be cultivated even in such a rural area. She begins doing watercolors and succeeds in marketing them with a dealer in New York. The heavy-handed morals of the story are that "a girl who makes the best of things in one place, will do it in every place," and "there is certainly a great difference between making life and taking it."

This story, more perhaps than others, reveals Sarah's own situation with respect to her family and the rural environment of South Berwick, set in opposition to the excitement and sophistication of Boston where by now she had many friends and had spent much time. Like Annie Hollis she had to deal with the boredom and poverty of rural living, and like her too she found a solution in her art, which became a way for her to bridge the two cultures. She would use the rural world in her literature, which she would market in the city. Jewett's ambivalence toward rural society and the curious outsider status she held regarding it are marked throughout her early work. It is especially noticeable in *Deephaven* where the unresolved tension becomes obtrusive enough to mar the work.

Another early story, however, "A Bit of Shore Life" (*Atlantic Monthly* August 1879, *Old Friends and New* 1879), is where we find Jewett's harshest condemnation of the limitations of country life, and the clearest sense of her own impatience with its spiritual poverty. From it we may conclude that

Jewett's moralistic urgings to do the best with one's lot were not her only opinion on the subject, and that perhaps the moralizing was at least partially designed to keep herself from despair.

"A Bit of Shore Life" is a remarkable story and one of the first to describe the seacoast area of southern Maine. Some of the imagery in this story is characteristic of Jewett's developed style at its most exquisite, as, for example, the following description of an early morning by the sea: "The world was just then like the hollow of a great pink sea-shell; and we could only hear the noise of it, and the dull sound of the waves among the outer ledges."

The narrator is a Jewett persona who has a regional dialect. (This becomes one of the distinctions between outsiders and locals in Jewett's fictional world. The insiders speak in dialect. The visitors do not. Later Jewett personae do not use dialect, which perhaps indicates a shift in her own self-image.) The other characters are Georgie, a taciturn youth, his father, and Georgie's unmarried aunts, Hannah and Cynthia West, who live together "up country."

The story's main event is a day-long trip the narrator and Georgie take to visit the sisters. On the way they pass by an auction where the Widow Wallis is selling a lifetime's accumulation of household items before moving to the city to live with her son. It is clear she is doing this with great reluctance. The scene is presented with considerable pathos but also with a sense of irony at the paltry life the widow is sorry to leave.

In this episode, Jewett's perception of the boredom and pettiness of rural society is unusually acute.

It is most noticeable among the elderly women. Their talk is very cheerless, and they have a morbid interest in sicknesses and deaths. . . . They are very forlorn; they dwell persistently upon any troubles which they have; and their

petty disputes with each other have a tragic hold upon
their thoughts, sometimes being handed down from one
generation to the next. Is it because their world is so small,
and life affords so little amusement and pleasure, and is at
best such a dreary round of the dullest housekeeping?

Here Jewett approaches the vision of her sister New
England author Mary E. Wilkins Freeman.

When the travelers finally reach the West home,
they find it to be similarly disappointing. One sister,
Hannah, is however of the Jewett breed of activists
who make do. She was "a tall, large woman, who had
a direct businesslike manner, —what the country
people would call a master smart woman, or a regular driver." She had worked for a while in the city as
a teacher and then a tailoress.

Her sister, Cynthia, on the other hand, is an
example of one who has given in to her surroundings. She is incapable and childlike. Her "chief pride
and glory was a silly little model of a house . . . ." But
tears come to the narrator's eyes at the "thought of
this poor, plain woman, who has such a capacity for
enjoyment, and whose life had been so dull . . . . "

The other stories in *Play Days* reflect the themes
we have discussed to this point. Indeed the collection is prefaced by a poem, "Discontent" (*St. Nicholas*
February 1876, *Play Days* 1878, *Verses* 1916), which
describes a buttercup that is urged to stop wishing
itself a daisy, to be content with its own nature. The
poem sets the collection's keynote of making do with
circumstances.

"The Water Dolly" (*St. Nicholas* December 1873)
deals with a poor rural child, Prissy, who finds a doll
in the tide and wants to keep it. Her father insists,
however, that they try to find the owner, which they
do at a nearby hotel. The owner is a rich girl who
after understanding the situation generously gives
the doll to Prissy. Prissy's story is continued in

"Prissy's Visit" (*The Independent* 7 January 1875) whose moral is to make do with little pleasures.

"Patty's Dull Christmas" (*The Independent* 23 December 1875) urges a similar point. Patty is invited to spend Christmas with her elderly aunts in Boston. She doesn't want to go, but her father says that the greatest happiness comes from doing good for others. Patty decides to go, and she has a wonderful time after all and learns that her father's dictum is true.

Both "My Friend the Housekeeper" (*St. Nicholas* September 1874) and "Marigold House" (*St. Nicholas* July 1875) concern a wealthy girl, Nelly Ashford, who has been given a large playhouse. The second story presents the masquerade theme: Nelly pretends to be Queen Victoria and is visited by a Widow Sullivan who speaks with a thick brogue. (This may be the first time Jewett attempted to use Irish dialect in the dialogue of her stories.) It turns out that the widow is her Aunt Bessie in disguise, playing a joke on Nelly.

"Nancy's Doll" (*The Independent* 31 August 1876) is one of the more interesting of the *Play Days* stories, for it gives us a glimpse of nineteenth-century urban poverty, probably that of Boston. Nancy is an extremely poor child who is meagerly supported by her aunt in a tenement house. "In old times one rich family had lived there, instead of four or five poor ones." Nancy is shy and lame and has but one wish in the world: to own a battered-up old doll she notices in a nearby shop window. It costs seven cents, which is way beyond their means. When Nancy asks her aunt for the money, she snaps at the child that "they would be lucky to keep from starving and freezing in such hard times."

One day a wealthy young woman from the country happens to pass through in her coach (Jewett?), takes pity on the girls in the street and gives each of them a five-cent piece. Unfortunately, however, now that Nancy has almost enough money for the doll, she becomes grievously ill. The money has to be spent on medicine.

Another wealthy angel of charity, Miss Helen, appears on the scene at this point to nurse Nancy. Helen buys her the doll and contacts a competent physician, who sends Nancy to Children's Hospital. The doctor even indicates that it may be possible to cure her lameness. The story thus ends happily through the agency of the charitable wealthy woman. This sentimental story expresses a certain historical accuracy, for what today we would call social work or welfare work was in the nineteenth century conceived as charity work that leisure class women undertook as a Christian duty. Jewett's close friend Annie Fields was a leader in this field in Boston. She was director of Associated Charities of Boston for many years and wrote a book on the subject, *How to Help the Poor*, in 1883.

Deephaven was Jewett's first major work. It is the most highly regarded of her early compositions; it has been reprinted many times (as recently as 1966) and continues to be the subject of critical commentary. Although flawed, it remains of considerable historical and literary value. It is not, however, as strong a work as *Old Friends and New,* Jewett's other major collection of the seventies. Jewett's standards in several of the *Old Friends and New* stories— especially "Miss Sydney's Flowers," "A Lost Lover," "A Late Supper" and "A Bit of Shore Life"— were extremely high.

Nevertheless, *Deephaven* remains of great interest for several reasons. First, it continues to develop several of the themes that appear in *Play Days* and investigates new issues that were to become important in Jewett's subsequent works. Second, the

structural problems in the work are indicative of
conflicting viewpoints toward her subject matter
and her art that existed within Jewett herself and
that needed to be resolved. Third, it describes ex-
tensively and realistically the seacoast region that
was to become Jewett's favorite locale. If only for its
extraordinary veracity of detail *Deephaven* still de-
serves to be read. In this regard it has the value of
charming and well-edited oral history. Nineteenth-
century daily life comes alive in this work as it does in
few others.

Because of its extraordinary sense of verisimilitude, there has been considerable speculation
as to where *Deephaven* is really set. Its setting seems
to resemble York, Maine, a coastal town about ten
miles from South Berwick. Especially suggestive is
the author's reference to the "cliffs and pebble
beaches, the long sands and the short sands," terrain
characteristic of York. However, in her preface to
the second edition of *Deephaven* (1893), Jewett insisted that it was a "fictitious village which still exists
only in the mind." This was a position she was to take
in regard to all her fiction.

This analysis of *Deephaven* proceeds more or less
in order of composition. Like most of Jewett's
fiction, these sketches were first published in
magazine form and later collected. Unlike most of
her other collections (with the notable exception of
The Country of the Pointed Firs), Jewett attempted in
revising these sketches for book publication to fuse
them together into a form that would approach the
coherence and design of a novel. This attempt was
not entirely successful. These sketches do not form a
continuous pattern: rather, they remain isolated
units only loosely and roughly connected. The main
reason for this is that they were written at different
times and only later patched together into a con-

tinuous fabric. By contrast, *The Country of the Pointed Firs, Deephaven's* more mature structural analogue, seems to have been composed in reverse order: first written all of a piece and then later divided for serial presentation.

The work's other major structural problem stems from Jewett's attempt to use the relationship between the two young women as the central unifying device. The only continuity in the work (other than the geographic unity forced by the location) is provided by the continuing presence through all the sketches of the two friends, Kate Lancaster and Helen Denis. The latter is the narrator and a Jewett persona.

For the most part these protagonists remain outsiders to the events and characters of the sketches. They do not participate in the action or the world of the text, nor is their relationship with one another integrated into that world. Indeed, the sentimentality of their liaison and their adolescent enthusiasm clash with the mood of their somber environment.

There is, however, one important connection between the girls and the environment: they learn from it. Their surroundings provide several important educational experiences for them that are especially related to their growth into adult women. The work might thus be seen as an embryonic *Bildungsroman,* or novel of education, a form Jewett was to use in *A Country Doctor* (1884). However, the time period covered (one summer) is too short for the work to be considered seriously as a novel of this genre.

By the end of the work the girls express an escapist wish, to "copy the Ladies of Llangollen and remove ourselves from society and its distractions." The Ladies of Llangollen, Lady Eleanor Butler and

Miss Sarah Ponsonby, were a celebrated lesbian couple of the late eighteenth and early nineteenth centuries who lived much of their life together in a Welsh rural retreat. Here perhaps most clearly we see that the escapist theme that recurs in Jewett's work (the desire to remain in a state of perpetual childhood or to retreat into some woodland haven) probably reflects a desire not to have to conform to the role demands that "adulthood" required in Victorian America.

Consequently, *Deephaven* is in reality made up of two separate texts that do not fit together well. One is the romantic/escapist story of the girls' relationship, and the other is the description of a nineteenth-century New England port village that is suffering an economic decline. Thus, *Deephaven* remains an inconsistent work that reflects its author's conflicting aims. On the one hand, she wished to create a work that would memorialize a valued personal relationship. This is demonstrated by the biographical evidence presented in Chapter I and also by Jewett's own secretive dedication of the 1877 edition: to her parents "and also to all my other friends, whose names I say to myself lovingly, though I do not write them here." On the other hand, she was motivated by a desire to preserve in fiction the beloved regional locale that was fast giving way to the modern world.

This conflict was resolved in Jewett's later work by simply removing personal matters like Helen's and Kate's relationship from her fiction. Most of Jewett's later narrator/visitors have little or no personal life (or at least the reader learns nothing about it). The last work that was seriously autobiographical was *A Country Doctor* (to be discussed in the next chapter). It seems to have provided its author with a sufficient outlet, so that she no longer needed to

treat personal concerns in her fiction. Or perhaps
she felt unable to deal with intimate subjects on the
same level of artistic sophistication at which she
handled more removed topics. Probably the fact
that Jewett's personal life was pretty well anchored
in Boston by the mid-1880s made it easier for her to
treat her local "homeland" with the distance of a
foreign observer. Therefore it became easier to treat
such material "aesthetically"—with an eye to its
fictional value rather than to its personal, moral
significance.

The first two sketches in *Deephaven*, "Kate
Lancaster's Plan" and "The Brandon House and the
Lighthouse," were originally published as "The
Shore House" (*Atlantic Monthly* September 1873).
The story opens in Boston when Kate Lancaster
proposes to her friend Helen Denis that they spend
the summer in Deephaven at the beach home of her
recently deceased aunt, Katherine Brandon. This
agreed, the two proceed by rail and by stagecoach to
their destination. In the coach they meet their first
local "character," Mrs. Kew, who has lived with her
husband, the lighthouse keeper, in the lighthouse
for seventeen years. (It seems likely that this is the
still much photographed Nubble Light on Cape
Neddick, Maine.) Mrs. Kew speaks in "downeast' "
dialect, as do all the characters in the work except
the girls.

After getting settled in the Brandon House,
which from its description strongly resembles
Jewett's own house in South Berwick, the two go to
visit the Kews in the lighthouse. While there, some
tourists stop by and mistake the girls for natives.
Kate plays the part of tour guide, another example
of the masquerade theme. Ironically, one of the
tourists takes pity on her, seeing Kate's lighthouse
life as one of loneliness and poverty, and suggests

that she move to the city where she could obtain a well-paid position such as department store saleswoman (a job she, the tourist, holds). This is a comically ironic reversal of the usual Jewett situation, with in this case the outsider being mistaken for the insider and the wealthy person for the poor. It betrays once again Jewett's concern about, or at least interest in, these social roles and the "masquerades" they require.

The next sketch, "My Lady Brandon and the Widow Jim," was probably written in 1873 but not published until it was included in *Deephaven*. The narrative structure of this story is especially interesting. It proceeds by means of conversations between Kate, Helen, and Mrs. Patton, the "widow Jim," who takes over the narrative for much of the story. She tells the girls much local lore and especially about Aunt Katherine, who had been her wealthy neighbor for decades.

Mrs. Patton is another Jewett character who possesses "the art of telling a story capitally." She sprinkles her narrative with lively expressions ("Land o'compassion!") and vivid imagery ("I've got as many roots as the big ellum"). In describing a favorite mug she notes:

My grand'ther Joseph Toggerson—my mother was a Toggerson—picked it up on the long sands in a wad of sea-weed: strange it wasn't broke but it's tough; I've dropped it on the floor, many's the time, and it ain't even chipped. There's some Dutch reading on it and it's marked 1732.

This kind of precise description, first fully developed in *Deephaven*, is one of the hallmarks of Jewett's style. It seems at times as if she had merely tape-recorded local narratives, so faithfully do these descriptions seem to represent the "real" world of

Deephaven. Jewett once commented, however, that only one of the Deephaven characters, Miss Chauncey, was taken from real life.

The widow Jim's own story is not entirely a happy one. She is the first of a long line of Jewett women who have been left economically stranded by incompetent husbands, a situation not uncommon in nineteenth-century America. The girls are clearly intended to learn from her experience; this is one of the occasions in which the work takes on the format of the education novel.

Mrs. Patton relates her story as follows:

Mr. Patton,—that was my husband,—he owned a good farm there when I married him, but I come back here after he died; place was all mortgaged. I never got a cent, and I was poorer than when I started. I worked harder'n ever I did before or since to keep things together, but 'twasn't any kind o' use. . . . I come back here a widow and destitute, and I tell you the world looked fair to me when I left this house first to go over there.

And she points out the moral to her listeners: "Don't you run no risks, you're better off as you be, dears"—a straightforward indictment of marriage, one of the life options the girls surely were contemplating.

The sketch concludes on a grim note. Another neighbor, Mrs. Dockum, tells the girls that the widow's plight was even worse than she had described: she had been a victim of wife abuse.

Dreadful tough time of it with her husband, shif'less and drunk all the time. Noticed that dent in the side of her forehead, I s'pose? That's where he liked to have killed her; slung a stone bottle at her.

The girls are appropriately shocked.

The next two sketches, "Deephaven Society" and "The Captains" were originally published, together with "Danny," "The Circus at Denby" and "Last Days in Deephaven" as "Deephaven Cronies" (*Atlantic Monthly* September 1875). Perhaps the best description of the town is to be found in "Deephaven Society." We learn that it "is utterly out of fashion. It never recovered from the effects of the embargo of 1807, and a sand bar has been steadily filling in the mouth of the harbor." In this sketch, too, we find the girls' sense of themselves as cultured "outsiders" at perhaps its most pronounced. "There was a great deal of sea lingo in use; indeed we learned a great deal ourselves . . . and used it afterward to the great amusement of our friends."

"The Captains" introduces a series of retired sea captains and mates who relate their stories to the girls. Especially interesting in this sketch is Captain Lant's story of a psychic phenomenon: how his step-father had once dreamed of his nephew being hung, which he later found out had happened on the other side of the world on the very same day as the dream. The central figure of the next sketch, "Danny," is a sailor who relates a touching and pathetic story about his long-term relationship with a cat he had once rescued. "Captain Sands," which follows "Danny" in *Deephaven* but which had not been published previously, introduces a character who is the protagonist of a later sketch, "Cunner-Fishing."

"The Circus at Denby" is one of the most interesting sketches in the book. Helen and Kate accompany Mrs. Kew to the circus, which has set up its tents in a nearby town. On the way they pass by red-bearded, consumptive Mr. Craper (a figure out of Dostoevsky) and his five children. They too are going to the circus, despite his obvious ill health. The circus turns out to be somewhat disillusioning; it is shabby and the animals look uncomfortable. The central figure of the sketch is "the Kentucky giantess," the fat lady in the side show. It happens that Mrs. Kew had known the woman in her youth. Her story is another tale of an incompetent, drunk husband. She has turned to her current profession as a means of supporting herself. "She used to be real ambitious," Mrs. Kew comments dismally on their way home. Once again the girls are presented with a grim example of the fate of a married woman.

That evening the two girls go to a free lecture on the "Elements of True Manhood." The main point of the lecture—that young men should exercise their duties and responsibilities as citizens and voters—is largely lost on the audience, which is composed of three old men, four women, two adolescent girls, four children, and "the sexton, a deaf little old man with a wooden leg." Women of course were not considered citizens and did not have the right to vote until the twentieth century.

"Cunner-Fishing" delves further into the question of psychic phenomena. Captain Sands tells the girls of four separate occurrences he knows in which people have anticipated or learned of events through extrasensory perception. Kate and Helen reflect upon how country people seem to be more in tune with their spiritualistic instincts than city dwellers. "They believe in dreams, and they have a kind of fetichism, and believe so heartily in supernatural causes." Helen speaks of having a certain reverence for this side of their lives: "They live so much nearer to nature than [city] people. . . . I wonder if they are unconsciously awed by the strength and purpose in the world about them, and the mysterious creative power which is at work with them on their familiar farms."

In their simple life they take their instincts for truths, and perhaps they are not always so far wrong as we imagine.

Because they are so instinctive and unreasoning, they may have a more complete sympathy with Nature.

Kate remarks that "the more one lives out of doors the more personality there seems to be in what we call inanimate things." Captain Sands had suggested that our psychic powers are really in an embryonic state; he had drawn an analogy to a tadpole's legs, which are useless "faculties" until it becomes a frog. So too, he speculated, our psychic faculties may in some future state find their use.

The last three sketches, "Mrs. Bonny," "In Shadow," and "Miss Chauncey" were originally published together as "Deephaven Excursions" (*Atlantic Monthly* September 1876). Mrs. Bonny is one of Jewett's great characters. A tobacco-smoking country woman who wears men's clothes and boots, several layers of aprons, a tight cap and "steel-bowed" spectacles, she is an original, uncontaminated by the civilized world. Kate and Helen visit her in her mountain home which is filled with "a flock of hens and one turkey."

Living there in the lonely clearing, deep in the woods and far from any neighbor, she knew all the herbs and trees and the harmless wild creatures who lived among them, by heart; and she had an amazing store of tradition and superstition.

Mrs. Bonny is an archetypal Jewett figure, the single woman who is in tune with nature and who has an extensive knowledge of herbal and natural lore. While presented in a somewhat comic vein here, she prefigures Jewett's monumental women, particularly Almira Todd of *The Country of the Pointed Firs.*

"In Shadow" presents a darker side of life, again the world of rural poverty. Here the characters are a poverty-stricken couple who die during

the summer, between the girls' two visits to their
home, leaving their children as orphans to be
farmed out to unwilling relatives (the alternative
being that nefarious nineteenth-century institution,
the "poorhouse"). These people are not "shif'less";
they simply had bad luck. As one neighbor remarked, " 'twas against wind and tide with 'em all
the time."

The two girls' responses to this example of inexplicable misery and suffering differ. Kate gleans a
Christian moral, but Helen meditates, "I wonder
how we can help being conscious in the midst of our
comforts and pleasures, of the lives which are being
starved to death in more ways than one." This comment is probably a fair expression of Jewett's own
developing attitude toward her rural environment;
it is one of compassion.

"Miss Chauncey" describes another life that
faded from an early promise to an impoverished
end. The central figure is an aristocratic old woman
from a distinguished but mad family (one of her
brothers had committed suicide, another had gone
insane). She lost her own bearings at one point, was
institutionalized for a while and then returned
home to find that all her belongings had been sold.
She lived for years in an empty house, half crazy,
dreaming of the past. The girls visit her several
times and then learn, after leaving Deephaven, that
Miss Chauncey had died while revisiting her house,
unbeknownst to anyone, in the dead of winter.
Deephaven thus follows the cycle of the year, beginning in a season of promise, early summer, and
ending in winter. In the meantime, the girls have
learned much.

Deephaven was not greeted by critical acclaim.
The worst review Jewett was ever to receive appeared in the *New York Times* of 28 April 1877. It
sourly observed: "It is by some mistake, doubtless,

that it got in print at all."[4] However, William Dean
Howells in the *Atlantic Monthly* noted "a fresh and
delicate quality" in the sketches. "We cannot express
too strongly the sense of conscientious fidelity which
the art of the book gives, while over the whole is cast
a light of the sweetest and gentlest humor."[5] The
Eclectic reviewer also remarked upon its "Pre-
Raphaelite fidelity and minuteness of detail" and its
"delicacy of touch."[6]

Happily the reviews of *Old Friends and New* were
even more enthusiastic. One reviewer stated, "her
stories [are] nearly perfect in their way."[7] "Miss
Sydney's Flowers" (*The Independent* 16 July 1874, *Old
Friends and New* 1879), the first of these "nearly
perfect" stories to be written, ranks with the best of
Jewett's work.

Miss Sydney, one of Jewett's "maiden lady"
figures, is the last in a distinguished old family line.
Her home is the last of its kind standing. "One by
one the quiet, aristocratic old street had seen its
residences give place to shops and warehouses...."
Once again we see quality and uniqueness giving
way to industrialization and mass production, a
perennial Jewett lament. As the story opens, Miss
Sydney's environment is about to be even more
abused, as a new commercial street is being put in
behind it. At first Miss Sydney resents the intrusion
the bustling traffic brings into her quiet space.
However, even these miserable new circumstances
have their positive side: it turns out that the crowds
of people passing by are attracted to the beautiful
flowers growing in her greenhouse, an event that
tends to break into the isolation of this lonely spinster who had heretofore kept "selfishly" to herself.
It forces her back into human society.

A parallel plot is developed in the second part of
the story. Here we see the underside of life again,
the world of urban poverty. Mrs. Marley, a candy

saleswoman, has earned barely enough to support herself and her lame sister Polly. Her candy stand had been located where the winter winds had harshly aggravated her rheumatism. With the advent of the new avenue that goes by Miss Sydney's, however, Mrs. Marley is able to relocate to a position that makes business much brisker and the task much pleasanter, as it is well sheltered from the winds. The location is in front of Miss Sydney's, beside the greenhouse. The sister, Polly, is another example of the Jewett character who makes do with meager pleasures (she cares for a crippled pigeon on her window ledge, for example.)

At first Miss Sydney resents the commercial enterprise Mrs. Marley has brought to her corner. Eventually, however, she takes pity on the woman, invites her in, learns of her dire situation, and offers the sisters substantial financial help. Miss Sydney learns to be unselfish and charitable late in life, and the moral of the story is that the "seeds of kindness and charity and helpfulness began to show themselves above the ground in the almost empty garden of her heart." Although it is openly moralistic, this story succeeds even for the modern reader; it approaches the power and pathos of a Tolstoy moral tale.

"A Lost Lover" (*Atlantic Monthly* March 1878, *Old Friends and New* 1879) is perhaps less successful—it is marred by a highly improbable coincidence —but it nevertheless remains a significant and charming story. Horatia Dane, another end-of-the-line spinster, who is, however, "not unhappy in her loneliness," is rumored by village gossips to have lost a lover in her youth. Nelly, a twenty-year-old relative, comes for an extended visit with Horatia. Nelly naturally sentimentalizes the story of the lost romance, but it is clear that Jewett (and Horatia her-

self) senses that the old woman was probably better
suited to spinsterhood than wifedom. (The story
thus shares some of the elements of Mary E. Wilkins
Freeman's classic, "A New England Nun.") That her
fate could have been much worse is clear when an
alcoholic "tramp" appears at the door one day, begging for a meal. It turns out that this is the old lover,
who had been shipwrecked while a youth and
rescued by a disease-ridden Chinese junk. He barely
survived this, only to be captured by a pirate ship
that held him for thirty years. He also abandoned a
wife (and presumably children) in Australia in the
course of his adventures.

As the tramp tells his story, Horatia recognizes
him but manages to keep her head. She sends him on
his way with a generous gift of ten dollars. After his
departure she faints, but no one else learns of his
identity, and he fortunately does not recognize her.
Here again we have the characteristic Jewett pattern
of the worthless husband and the resourceful and
successful single woman. Also characteristic are the
details of the sea adventure, which Jewett undoubtedly modeled on the many such yarns she had heard
in her childhood.

Like "Miss Sydney's Flowers" and many other
Jewett stories, "A Lost Lover" is also noteworthy for
its precise descriptions of vegetation and domestic
gardening practices.

The green peas were all shelled presently. . . . The sun
would not be round that side of the house for a long time
yet, and the pink and blue morning-glories were still in
their full bloom and freshness. They grew over the window, twined on strings exactly the same distance apart.
There was a box crowded full of green houseleeks down at
the side of the door: they were straying over the edge, and
Melissa stooped stiffly down with an air of disapproval at
their untidiness. ". . . [Horatia's] mother she set every

thing by 'em. She fetched 'em from home with her when she was married, her mother kep' a box, and they came from England. Folks used to say they was good for bee-stings."

"A Late Supper" (*Sunday Afternoon* January 1878, *Old Friends and New* 1879) is set in Brockton, a country town which is "like any other town, a minia-ture world, with its great people and small people, bad people and good people, its jealousy and rivalry, kindness and patient heroism." Again the heroine, Miss Catherine Spring, is a spinster who is some-times lonely but who knows, "it is, after all, a great satisfaction to do as one pleases."

Catherine has run into financial difficulties (the railroad she had invested in has failed to pay its dividends), so she is facing the prospect of having to sell her house. While she is lamenting this, Katy, a neighbor girl, comes to the door and asks for work. Catherine gives her some cream and some special cake that she has made, but is unable to hire her.

Meanwhile her nephew from the city, his wife, and her friend arrive unexpectedly for dinner. Since she has given all her cream to the little girl, Catherine has to run over to a neighbor's to borrow more for dinner. On the way events occur that, while highly improbable on the surface, are both propiti-ous for Catherine and highly comic for the reader. They therefore seem believable within the comic and benign world of this charming story.

The neighbors live on the other side of a rail-road track. This presents no problem on Catherine's trek to their farm. On the return, however, she finds that a train has stalled on the tracks and blocked her way. Because she is anxious to return to her dinner and her guests, Catherine jumps on the train, hop-ing to step down on the other side quickly. Just as she does so, however, the train starts up. So there she is, caught on a train in her housedress, holding a pitcher of cream. Fortune is with her, however; on the train she encounters Alice West and her aunt. They are traveling north to spend the summer as boarders near the mountains. In the course of the conversation Catherine mentions her financial plight and how she saw taking in boarders as one solution. They all lament that they hadn't met earlier: the Wests could have boarded with her. Catherine gets off at the next stop and takes a return train back to her home, arriving just in time for "a late supper." Shortly thereafter she receives a letter from Alice stating that they are dissatisfied with the lodgings they had procured and wonder if they could stay with Catherine for the summer. This resolves the story happily. Catherine is even able to hire Katy to help with the new boarders.

While the tale is highly comic in tone—there is even an element of farce in the train scene—one is tempted to analyze it seriously. Clearly Catherine is a victim of the economic vagaries of industrial capitalism. The strong and nefarious presence of the railroad in the story accentuates this theme. By a stroke of fortune in combination with her own resourcefulness she is able to triumph over her fate. There is a fairy-tale quality about this story that perhaps reflects its author's wish that the small business people of the world win their way against its controlling corporate powers.

The two remaining stories in *Old Friends and New,* "A Sorrowful Guest" (*Sunday Afternoon* July 1879) and "Lady Ferry" (not published previously), return to Jewett's interest in the supernatural. Neither is entirely successful. "A Sorrowful Guest" is a Hawthorne-like mystery involving the visit of an old classmate, Whiston, to the Boston home of John

Ainslie, who lives with his sister Helen. Whiston has "monomania," which means he sees things that aren't there. Specifically, in the drawing room he sees the "ghost" of his friend Dunster, who had been killed in the Civil War. Thus haunted, Whiston soon dies, after which Ainslie encounters Dunster, who is alive in a veteran's hospital. Apparently at least once (in Rio de Janeiro) Whiston had actually seen Dunster since the war, and this had started his "monomania." Dunster is presented as a rather despicable character, although his persecution of Whiston is largely inadvertent. The story is a reasonable example of the suspense genre, but is interesting only insofar as it shows that Jewett was trying her hand at a variety of genres.

"Lady Ferry," which is also not a first-rate story, is nevertheless much more interesting than "A Sorrowful Guest." Howells rejected the story for the *Atlantic Monthly*, but Jewett stuck by it and included it in *Old Friends and New*. This practice of "floating" previously rejected stories in collections of published stories was one in which Jewett occasionally indulged, most notably later with her celebrated "A White Heron." Time has not borne out her faith in "Lady Ferry," however. It is too long and once again suffers from a clash in mood between the young naive narrator's viewpoint and the grim supernatural happenings at the home she is visiting. There lives the character called Lady Ferry, a wandering-Jew figure, who is, according to local lore, condemned to immortality. The young girl meets this elderly woman and tries not to be intimidated. But strange things happen: one night the girl thinks she sees a strange party going on with Lady Ferry as the hostess to historical figures. She sees some of them leave by boat. Was it a dream? The next morning it turns out that the boats are missing.

These events are not further explained. As an adult, the young girl returns to the home to find that Lady Ferry did finally die. Her grave is marked, so she was not truly immortal. Was it a child's overheated imagination that painted the nocturnal picture, or is it that children, like country people, are closer to the world of the spiritual? Jewett leaves this question unanswered.

3

City versus Country:
1880–1886

The central dilemma in Sarah Orne Jewett's life and in her fiction during the early 1880s continued to be the conflicting attractions of rural and of urban life. It was during this period that she established what was to be a lifelong living arrangement with Annie Adams Fields in Boston. Since she also retained her home in South Berwick, she was able to keep involved in both worlds, rural and urban. By mid-decade, she seems to have arrived, therefore, at a practical solution to the conflict. Her personal integration of the conflicting worlds of the country and the city is reflected in the ending of *A Country Doctor* (1884). In that work, Nan Prince, the protagonist, is also able to achieve a creative integration of her urban, professional self and her rural identity. The question is also a central issue in Jewett's other novel of the period, *A Marsh Island* (1885). The rural–urban conflict culminates in her classic story, "A White Heron," where it found its most complex and moving expression.

This period of Jewett's writing includes, in addition to the two novels, three collections of short stories: *Country By-Ways* (1881), which was dedicated to her father; *The Mate of the Daylight, and Friends Ashore* (1884), which was dedicated to Annie Fields, and *A White Heron and Other Stories* (1886), dedicated to her older sister, Mary Rice Jewett. Aside from the works that deal with the rural–urban conflict, the stories fall into several groupings. One set focuses on the issue of role reversal; another is a series of country sketches. A third group includes several of Jewett's classic spinster tales, and a fourth focuses on father–child relationships.

"Stolen Pleasures" (unidentified Canadian newspaper c. 1880, *Uncollected Stories* 1971) is the first of Jewett's stories to be set within a relationship, in this case a marriage, and to deal with the questions of gender role expectations. John Webber, the main character, from whose point of view the story is told, is a worker at Zenith Machine Company. The story opens as John is returning home one evening with a secret to tell his wife: he has been granted a two-week vacation starting the next day. Ironically, she, however, has left that morning for the seashore with her baby and her worldly friend, Nell Stince. John is severely depressed by this and calls the friend a bad influence on Hattie for having encouraged her to be too independent and "selfish." John retreats to his mother who chastises him for keeping his vacation a secret from Hattie, counseling him to treat her more like an equal in the future. "Don't you think everything's as *you* say. She's got rights an' you've been too good sometimes, and treated her an' the baby just the same way other times." Meanwhile Hattie is having a miserable time at the seashore and repents her rebelliousness. So they reconcile and resolve to behave more maturely in the future.

"Hallowell's Pretty Sister" (*Good Company* No. 9 1880, *Uncollected Stories* 1971) deals more directly with gender role reversal but treats the subject comically. Classmates from Dick Hallowell's school visit his home. Jack Spenser, the "lady's man" in the group, falls for Hallowell's "sister," Alice, in reality

Dick's fifteen-year-old brother Tom, who is talented at mimicry and who specializes in female parts in school plays. When the real Alice shows up, the masquerade is exposed to great laughter.

Perhaps the most hilarious of the stories of this genre is "An Autumn Holiday" (*Harper's Magazine* October 1880, *Country By-Ways* 1881). Originally entitled "Miss Daniel Gunn," the story has as its central figure a transvestite. Daniel Gunn is an elderly sea captain who "got sun-struck, and never was just right in his mind afterward." He decides that he is his sister Patience who had died several years previously. He begins wearing her clothes, and participating in such women's activities as the sewing bees of the Female Missionary Society. Neighbors humor him, because he has been a respected member of the community for years. Some of the local women even make him some dresses in his size—his sister's clothes had been a tight fit! One of the most farcical episodes is his appearance in meeting all dressed up in women's clothing. The parishioners cannot contain themselves but at the same time retain a sense of compassion for their old neighbor. The finale is the day the deacon comes calling. After his visit, Daniel asks his nephew if he thinks the deacon (who is a widower) seems interested in him romantically. Thus the role reversal is complete; "Miss Gunn," a rough old sea captain, is eager to play courted maiden.

The roundabout narrative structure of this story is an interesting one, and a device Jewett used in several of her most successful stories. It opens with a young woman wandering in the country. After a long hike, during which the rural setting is described in great detail, she reaches an isolated home where Miss Polly Marsh and her sister, Mrs. Snow, sit spinning. They begin reminiscing about

various neighbors and finally tell the story of "Miss
Daniel Gunn."

The technique of including the tale within a
larger narrative is, of course, as old as literature.
One of the most memorable uses of this device was in
Cervantes's *Don Quixote de la Mancha,* in which the
knight and his squire, Sancho, continually encounter personages who relate their often comic
tales. The virtue of this technique is that it heightens
the reader's sense of verisimilitude. One of its draw-
backs, however, is that it sometimes allows for a
slackening of suspense. Jewett acknowledges in one
case that a particular character's "way of going
round Robin Hood's barn between the beginning of
her story and its end can hardly be followed at all,
and certainly not in her dear loitering footsteps"
("Miss Debby's Neighbors"). This is a criticism with
which Sancho would have heartily agreed, for he
often railed against long-winded narrative style.
Nevertheless, Jewett herself used her characters'
narrative vagaries for comic effect; only rarely, if
ever, does she lose aesthetic control of her material.

One other story of this period, "Tom's Husband" (*Atlantic Monthly* February 1882, *The Mate of
the Daylight 1884*), deals with role reversal within a
marriage. In this case the two main characters, Tom
Wilson, husband, and Mary Dunn, wife, find themselves temperamentally unsuited for the respective
marriage roles assigned them by convention. Mary is
"too independent and self-reliant for a wife; it
would seem at first thought that she needed a wife
herself more than she did a husband." Jewett's
feminist consciousness is apparent when she adds:
"Most men like best the women whose natures cling
and appeal to theirs for protection." Mary also has
great "executive ability" that is "often wasted in the
more contracted sphere of women." Tom, on the

other hand, decidedly lacks managerial ability, prefers a more traditionally female style for himself, but likes his wife the way she is.

For financial reasons the family needs to reopen their factory. Mary says she would much rather head the firm than do housework, which she considers her life's "great discipline." Tom jokingly says he would be much better at housework. Mary then seriously proposes that they switch roles. Tom finally agrees, remarking, "I'm the first man, apparently, who wished he were a woman." But Mary argues that it is only sensible to follow their own bents. Thus their experiment in role reversal begins. As time passes Mary develops attitudes characteristic of a businessman, and Tom those of a wife. She becomes disinterested in the housewifely trivia that comes to obsess Tom and becomes obsessed in her own right with business affairs. Finally, Tom begins to find his role too demeaning and calls a halt to the experiment.

. . . somehow he had an uneasy suspicion that she could get along pretty well without him when it came to the deeper wishes and hopes of her life. . . . He seemed to himself to have merged his life in his wife's; . . . he felt himself fast growing rusty and behind the times. . . . One day the thought rushed over him that his had been almost exactly the experience of most women, and he wondered if it really was any more disappointing and ignominious to him than it was to women themselves.

Jewett's recognition of the severe restrictions placed upon the married woman in the nineteenth century is quite apparent in this story. That these restrictions are ones she herself hoped to avoid becomes even clearer in her autobiographical novel *A Country Doctor*. Undoubtedly Jewett's fictional interest in role reversal stems from her own personal resistance to the traditional roles assigned to women in Victorian America.

Other stories in which Jewett consciously dealt with role reversal include "Farmer Finch" (*Harper's Magazine* January 1885, *A White Heron* 1886) and, less successfully, "The Stage Tavern" (*Youth's Companion* 12 April 1900, *Uncollected Stories* 1971). "Farmer Finch" describes a young woman who takes over management of a farm because her father is ill and otherwise incompetent. She makes a great success of her venture, much to everyone's surprise. In "The Stage Tavern," a recent Radcliffe graduate works competently as a tavern manager.

During the early 1880s Jewett also wrote a series of nonfictional sketches of rural settings. These she included in *Country By-Ways*. The first, "River Driftwood" (*Atlantic Monthly* October 1881, *Country By-Ways* 1881), describes the character and history of the Piscataqua River. "From A Mournful Villager" (*Atlantic Monthly* November 1881, *Country By-Ways* 1881) is an essay on front yards and gardens. "An October Ride" (*Country By-Ways* 1881) provides a sense of Jewett's feelings about nature. It describes a ride she had taken on her favorite chestnut horse, Sheila, through the countryside around South Berwick. In the course of the ride she experiences a transcendentalist meditation about the oneness of all existence.

I have no thought of the rest of the world. I wonder what I am; there is a strange self-consciousness, but I am only a part of one great existence which is called nature. The life in me is a bit of all life, and where I am happiest is where I find that which is next of kin to me, in friends, or trees, or hills, or seas, or beside a flower, when I turn back more than once to look into its face.

"A Winter Drive" (*Country By-Ways* 1881) is a similar

meditation, this time based on a winter drive she had taken up Mount Agamenticus near her home. A slightly later piece, "The Confession of A House-Breaker" (*The Mate of the Daylight* 1884), completes this series of essays. It describes an early morning walk in her garden.

This period also saw the creation of several of Jewett's best stories about New England spinsters. "Miss Becky's Pilgrimage" (*The Independent* 1 September 1881, *Country By-Ways* 1881) concerns Becky Parsons's return to her Maine home after a forty-year absence. She had spent most of her life in upstate New York caring for her recently deceased brother, the Reverend Parsons. Becky is apprehensive about her pilgrimage home, but on the train she encounters an old neighbor, Mahaly Robinson. Both secretly consider how decrepit the other looks but nevertheless are pleased to have a neighborly traveling companion. The story ends happily: Becky's relatives meet her at the train (she had feared they wouldn't), and shortly after, she meets an elderly preacher who proposes marriage.

Another classic, "A New Parishioner" (*Atlantic Monthly* April 1883, *The Mate of the Daylight* 1884) presents commonsensical Lydia Dunn who, though she lived alone, "always treated herself as if she were a whole family." The plot concerns the return home of an old parishioner, Henry Stroud, who has made his fortune in the South and now wishes to play town philanthropist. Everyone falls for him except Lydia who notes that he does not look people in the eye; she remembers that his father had once cheated her grandfather. Stroud's hypocrisy is finally revealed when it is discovered that he is wanted for fraud. The townspeople congratulate Lydia for her perspicacity, but she rejects their praise, noting the fickleness of village fancy: "First, folks was all pecking at me because I wouldn't bow down and worship him, and now they want me to throw rocks at his tomb-stone."

Another spirited spinster, Narcissa Manning, is the central figure in "Miss Manning's Minister" (*The Independent* 23 August 1883, *Uncollected Stories*, 1971), one of Jewett's first overtly anti-Calvinist stories. Narcissa "thought, contrary to Puritan tradition, it was no harm to heat whatever food she might happen to have; and she was obliged to confess that she always enjoyed the afternoon sermon more if she had a good, warm dinner." Miss Manning finds meaning in life by caring for Mr. Taylor, a minister who has recently returned from missionary work in India and had a stroke soon after. She is dismayed when he is taken to Boston for treatment, fearing she has lost him forever, but as he recovers he recognizes her kindness and rewards her devotion with an offer of marriage.

"Miss Debby's Neighbors" (*The Mate of the Daylight* 1884) is a rambling tale of family history told by Miss Debby, who regrets the passing of the preindustrial era. She had been a tailoress herself, but now that people were buying "cheap, ready-made-up clothes" her business has fallen off. "She always insisted . . . that the railroads were making everybody look and act of a piece, and that the young folks were more alike than people of her own day."

The White Heron and Other Stories includes five additional stories about unmated women. One, "Farmer Finch," was discussed earlier; another, "A White Heron," will be discussed below. The others are "Mary and Martha" (*The Christian Union* 26 November 1885), "The Dulham Ladies" (*Atlantic Monthly* April 1886), and "Marsh Rosemary" (*Atlantic Monthly* May 1886).

"Mary and Martha" is a disjointed story, one of the few Jewett pieces that lack thematic integrity. It concerns two sisters whose characters are modeled upon their Biblical counterparts. Mary is "Mary-like—a little too easy and loving-hearted; and Martha was Martha-like—a little too impatient with foolish folks, and forgetting to be affectionate while she tried to be what she called just." Jewett fails to connect this contrast of character to the plot of the story, which is that, being in financial straits, the sisters decide to invite a recently widowed wealthy cousin to Thanksgiving dinner. They hope to reap some financial gain from this gesture, but their motives are not entirely corrupt; they also wish to end a long-standing feud for reasons of Christian charity. They are successful, as the cousin offers them a sewing machine, which is just what they had needed to increase their income.

A much more successful story dealing with two sisters is "The Dulham Ladies," a much-anthologized tale. The story is highly comic, bordering on social satire, and reveals its author's impatience with social pretension.

To be leaders of society in the town of Dulham was as satisfactory to Miss Dobin and Miss Lucinda Dobin as if Dulham were London itself. . . . They were always conscious of the fact that they were the daughters of a once eminent Dulham minister.

Besides this "unanswerable claim" to social rectitude, their mother's grandmother was a "Greenaple of Boston." "Nothing can be finer than her account of having taken tea at Governor Clovenfoot's, on Beacon Street, in company with an English lord." ("Dulham," "Greenaple" and "Clovenfoot" are examples of a stylistic device rare in Jewett works, the name pun.)

The sisters' mother had made an unfortunate choice in marriage, their father. She married late and when she finally picked up "a crooked stick . . .

it made a great difference that her stick possessed an ecclesiastical bark." The Reverend Mr. Dobin was not only dull, he was a tyrant as well. But "providentially," he was "stopped short by a stroke of paralysis in the middle of his clerical career."

As time passes the Dobin sisters begin to imagine an even more prestigious ancestry: "The name was originally D'Aubigne, we think." But the younger parishioners persist in calling them "Dobbin." To attempt to retrieve some of their lost ascendency, the sisters decide to repair their looks by donning "frisettes," then-fashionable hairpieces worn over the forehead. Of course the neighbors are much amused, but in true Jewett fashion they treat the sisters with compassion rather than ridicule.

"Marsh Rosemary" is also about an elderly woman, but the tone of this story is one of pathos, not humor. It concerns a January–May romance between Miss Ann Floyd, a conscientious and responsible spinster, and Jerry Lane, who is young, irresponsible, and lazy. Nancy knows his faults, but the winters are long, cold, and lonely, so she agrees to marry him. Marriage proves burdensome to her, so it is not without relief that she learns of his plan to go to sea. Sometime later she hears that his ship has been lost and that she is a widow. Now she has "an ideal Jerry Lane to mourn over." Later, however, it transpires that he is alive and has remarried. Nancy decides to confront him with his bigamy, but on seeing him with his new wife and their infant child, she retreats home without saying anything, an old woman, pathetic and lonely.

Several stories from this period deal with a father–child theme, in particular that of the prodigal son. "Andrew's Fortune" (*Atlantic Monthly* July 1881, *Country By-Ways* 1881) is a lengthy story about a lost inheritance. Stephen Dennett, a wealthy landowner, had planned to make his adopted son, Andrew, his beneficiary, but the will was lost, so the inheritance went to distant and disagreeable relatives. All this proves to be a blessing in disguise, however, for Andrew moves to Boston, where he makes his fortune and marries a suitable wife. Later in life he returns to his father's farm and discovers the lost will. He burns it, however, since by now the relatives' children are enjoying the fruits of their mistaken inheritance.

"A Landless Farmer" (*Atlantic Monthly* May and June 1883, *Mate of the Daylight* 1884), as Jewett herself notes in the story, provides a combination of the King Lear and the prodigal son motifs. The story opens with Ezra Allen telling his neighbors of the despicable treatment his uncle, Jenkins, received from his daughter Serena and her husband Aaron Nudd. They have forced him to sign away his property to them and generally treat him as a nuisance who would be better off dead. The last straw occurs when Serena tells him that she has sold his ancient chest of drawers. He decides to leave and go live in town with another daughter, Mary Liddy Bryan. She is not much of a bargain either, being a notorious hypochondriac. Unlike *King Lear,* however, the story ends happily, as the prodigal son, Parker Jenkins, returns from successful gold mining in California to take on the responsibility of caring for the old man. Here we see what is perhaps characteristically American optimism, based on a faith in financial success, to transform a situation that has all the elements of grim tragedy. In later works Jewett's optimism is not so naive.

Another prodigal son tale with a happy ending is "An Only Son" (*Atlantic Monthly* November 1883, *Mate of the Daylight* 1884). A variation of the theme is also presented in the title story of *The Mate of the*

Daylight, in which Daniel Lewis proves himself to his elders on a transatlantic voyage as first mate of the *Daylight,* thus earning the right to marry his lover Susan.

Sarah Orne Jewett's first two novels, *A Country Doctor* and *A Marsh Island,* were apparently written at about the same time. Jewett noted in a letter to Annie Fields in June 1883 that she had just prepared two sections of *A Marsh Island* for the printer.[1] That novel was first published serially in 1885, while *A Country Doctor* appeared in 1884. Because *A Marsh Island* seems to precede *A Country Doctor* thematically, it will be treated first.

A Marsh Island is a pastoral romance set along the northern Massachusetts coast in Essex County between Newburyport and Manchester, near Annie Fields's summer home. Jewett once remarked that a glimpse of an island farm she once caught from a train gave her the idea for the setting.[2]

The plot concerns the courtship of a young country woman, Doris Owen, by two suitors; one is Dick Dale, a wealthy young man from the city who comes to the marsh area one summer to do a series of paintings. The other suitor is Dan Lester, a local boy. The novel opens with Dick painting the marshlands. As evening approaches, he seeks to spend the night at the farmhouse of Israel and Martha Owen and their daughter, Doris. He stays for several weeks. The Owenses' son, Israel Jr., had been killed in the Civil War. Dick uses his room and seems to resemble him. Doris, although quiet and somewhat shy, is a very competent person who drives her own horse and is considerably more skilled in physical farm labors than Dick.

Dan, on the other hand, is the sort of steady, dependable, salt-of-the-earth type who makes up in reliability what he lacks in glamor. He becomes jealous of Doris's apparent interest in Dick and begins to avoid her. In the meantime, Dan had made some money on a piece of Western land that had risen in value. This has enhanced his desirability as a mate, at least from Doris's parents' point of view. Dan finally comes round and proposes to Doris, but not before Dick has hinted at similar intentions. Doris is by this time pale and confused.

One day Dick's wealthy urban aunt, Mrs. Susan Winchester, happens to have carriage trouble near the farm. Dick agrees to drive her home after her victoria is repaired. This episode serves to remind Dick of his wealthy, urban origins, as the aunt chides him for seriously considering an involvement with a country girl and a change to rural life. She reminds him that he is destined for far greater things. He defends the honesty and simplicity of the farm people, but secretly realizes that her comments about his own future hold much truth.

Not long after this, Doris accompanies her father to deliver hay to a wealthy household on the coast. Seeing this estate makes her realize that this is Dick's natural environment but not hers. She in turn finds she feels a certain contempt for the rich and their "idle ways."

Dan, in the meantime, had become jealous again, after seeing Doris and Dick in a boat together. The Owenses learned one evening that he has decided to ship off on a schooner the next morning. Doris, who by now had made her choice, is panic-stricken. In the middle of the night she decides to go into town to plead with Dan before the boat sails. Her nocturnal journey across the marsh is described in suspenseful detail. Once in town she encounters Dan, who has already decided not to sail. But he realizes why she has undertaken her arduous trek and this suffices to prove her love for him once and

for all. Together they return to the farm, betrothed.
Everyone rejoices and Dick returns to the city. Later
they hear that he has successfully exhibited the
sketches he did that summer on Marsh Island.

This is the third time Jewett used the "two
suitors convention," the others being "Jenny
Garrow's Lovers" and "The Hare and the Tortoise"
(*Atlantic Monthly* August 1883). This fictional structure was pervasive in nineteenth-century novels
with female protagonists, as Jean E. Kennard has
demonstrated in her study, *Victims of Convention*.[3]
This convention provides the heroine with a choice
between two men, one of whom is "right" for her
and the other "wrong." In several Victorian novels,
including Mrs. Gaskell's *Mary Barton* (1848) the
suitors are from different classes; the wrong suitor is
aristocratic and the right suitor is of the working
class.[4] Jewett clearly followed this scheme in *A Marsh
Island*, but used it to her own purposes.

Significantly, in Jewett's handling of the convention, the aristocrat is associated with the city,
with wealth, and with intellectual and cultural opportunity; the working-class person is associated
with the country, with Spartan living, with simplicity
and honesty. Once again, therefore, in this novel, we
see the tension posed between urban and rural. The
two suitors represent a choice between two ways of
life. The implication in this novel is that one is destined, almost inherently, to live in one or the other
world, and that one must choose in accordance with
one's "natural" predisposition. Thus Dick returns to
his proper environs, and Doris chooses to remain in
hers.

Doris's mother is one who has never properly
adjusted to her rural environment, who continues to
pine after a world of greater excitement and opportunity, the city. The narrator seems ambivalent

toward this figure; on the one hand, there is sympathy:

Men folks were slow at understanding how a woman felt about such dull doings and lack of entertainment, the long winters and the endless, busy days of summer. She wished that Doris might be spared all this . . . .

On the other hand, there is chastisement. Martha Owen is a limited person who should be satisfied with her surroundings:

The Martha Owen of the Marsh Island would be the same in whatever scenes or circumstances she found herself, and not transformed to match her new vicinity. A good soul, but stationary, it was a great pity she had not been wise enough to love the place where she had been kindly planted.

But the situation with which Jewett herself must have had the most empathy was Dick's. For like Annie Hollis in "A Guest At Home," Dick has the difficult problem of loving the rural world but realizing the limitations it imposed on his own intellectual and artistic ambitions. This clearly was Jewett's own dilemma. Dick's choice of the city and professional development parallels Jewett's own decision.

Mrs. Winchester, Dick's aunt, is a new type in Jewett's repertoire of characters. She represents the haughty rich, those who do not genuinely understand the beauty and value of the rural world. She views it aesthetically, as charming and picturesque, but fails to realize the moral worth of its inhabitants. Jewett's condemnation of Mrs. Winchester's attitude is a significant step in the formulation of her own position toward her rural subjects. It suggests the unease that Jewett herself evidently felt about "using" her rural neighbors to further her own

literary ambitions, a posture Mrs. Winchester had
commended to Dick. Dick, however, represents a
more likable model, an artist who uses the rural
landscape to further his own success but who remains emotionally tied to that world. Significantly,
his chic urban friends, like Mrs. Winchester, ap-
preciate his aesthetic use of the countryside but do
not understand his emotional and moral identifica-
tion with it.

A Country Doctor is one of several American
novels written in the 1880s that have a woman physician as protagonist. William Dean Howells's *Dr.
Breen's Practice* (1881) presented the woman doctor
somewhat negatively, while Elizabeth Stuart Phelps
Ward and Louisa May Alcott both offered positive
images of the female doctor in *Dr. Zay* (1882) and *Jo's
Boys* (1886). Since the physician in Alcott's novel is
named Nan, as is the protagonist of *A Country Doctor*,
and since the plot outlines are somewhat similar (a
spinster who chooses career over marriage), Jewett's
work might have influenced Alcott.

It is unlikely, however, that the other novels of
the genre influenced Jewett, for her work is strongly
autobiographical. It is evident that the role of physician in the novel is really a cipher for the role of
artist, a full-time calling to which one dedicates one's
life. It is not surprising therefore that *A Country
Doctor* was Jewett's own favorite work.

The novel opens atypically, with a melodrama-
tic scene characteristic of the sentimental novel. A
woman carrying a child struggles across the countryside and collapses at nightfall on her parent's
doorstep. She is Adeline Thacher Prince, who had
"had a dreadful cravin' to be somethin' more'n
common," had left home years before to work in the
Lowell mills, and had married and been left a widow
with an infant. Within a few days of her arrival at

home she dies, leaving the child, Nan, an orphan, another feature borrowed from the sentimental novel. (There has been some speculation as to why so many women authors orphaned their female protagonists. Probably it was to allow them to grow "naturally" without undue parental socialization.)

True to form Nan grows up untrammeled by social convention. She is described as being wild, hard to handle, a child of nature. When Mrs. Thacher, her grandmother, dies, Dr. Leslie, a local physician, agrees to adopt her. Jewett acknowledged that she modeled Dr. Leslie on her own father; undoubtedly the relationship that develops between the youngster and the doctor was similar to that Sarah had with her father.

By the time Nan enters grammar school she has announced her ambition to become a doctor. The plot from this point on is constructed of a series of obstacles that threaten to deflect Nan from her life course. The first is Marilla, Dr. Leslie's maid, who had simply "laughed when she had been told of Nan's intentions, and had spoken disrespectfully of women doctors."

The next challenge is posed by Leslie's friend and college classmate, Dr. Ferris. In an after-dinner conversation the two discuss Nan's goals and the place of women professionals in general. Leslie declares that his philosophy of childrearing had been to let Nan grow "as naturally as a plant grows, not having been clipped back or forced in any unnatural direction." This is one of several organic metaphors in the novel, and it signals that the rationale that underlies Nan's unorthodoxy is that of transcendentalist or Romantic individualism. This philosophy holds that persons, like plants, are born with inherent designs or predispositions and that these talents must be allowed to unfold and to bloom freely if the

individual's destiny is to be realized. The transcendentalist Margaret Fuller's arguments for women's
rights followed essentially in this vein.

Dr. Ferris, after much protesting, finally comes
round to Leslie's point of view: "Do push your little
girl ahead if she has the real fitness. . . . The world
cannot afford to do without the workmen who are
masters of their business by divine right." Ferris
even refers to the work of Henry Thomas Buckle
(1821–1862), an English historian who had argued
that "the feminine intellect is the higher, and . . . the
great geniuses of the world have possessed it."

Dr Leslie has to summon up further arguments
to convince his neighbor Mrs. Graham of the right-
ness of his plan to send Nan to medical school. He
maintains once again that she is destined for a
career. "The law of her nature is that she must live
alone and work alone." She is not the "sort of girl
who will be likely to marry." "When a man or woman
has that sort of self-dependence and unnatural
self-reliance, it shows itself very early." And he adds
that Nan's feeling for her "boy-playmates is exactly
the same as toward the girls she knows." She does
not have the same "natural instinct toward marriage, and the building and keeping of a sweet
home-life" that many other young women of her age
have.

It is clear that Jewett is presenting the concept
of the professional woman as the exception, the extraordinary, almost the freak. Yet her plea is that
even these anomalies must be allowed to follow their
bents. As Leslie notes, "a rule is sometimes very
cruel for its exceptions; and there is a life now and
then which is persuaded to put itself in irons by the
force of custom and circumstances. . . ." He does not
wish this to happen to Nan.

Beyond the problem of social disapproval, however, lay the even thornier question of gender role

identity. For if Nan does not have the "natural" female instincts toward domesticity, is she something "unnatural"? Is she abandoning her female identity? Jewett answers this in the negative; Nan's school chums acknowledge that she

showed no sign of being the sort of girl who tried to be mannish and to forsake her natural vocation for a profession. She did not look strong-minded. . . . Yet everybody knew that she had a strange tenacity of purpose, . . . a lack of pretension, and [scorn for] the deceits of school-girl existence.

One senses that the dilemma for Nan, as perhaps for Jewett herself, was how to pursue a "male" profession and eschew the traditional roles of women while still retaining one's female identity and not adopting a male or "mannish" style.

Nan does, however, agree to delay entering medical school for a year or two after her graduation. During this time she becomes bored and restless, which tends to confirm for her and Dr. Leslie that she should commence her destined course. Once in medical school she meets overt discrimination.

If a young man plans the same course, everything conspires to help him and forward him. . . . But in the days of Nan's student life it was just the reverse. Though she had been directed toward such a purpose entirely by her singular talent, instead of by the motives of expediency which rule the decisions of a large proportion of the young men who study medicine, she found little encouragement either from the quality of the school, or the interest of society in general.

The final obstacle toward the realization of Nan's dreams comes during a vacation visit she makes to the home of her paternal aunt who has helped support her over the years. The aunt, Miss Prince, and a neighbor, Mrs. Fraley, are scandalized by her ambition. They argue that a woman's place is in the home, that it is unnatural for women to be so strong minded, and that a well-bred girl should not go into medicine. All of these arguments Nan rebuts.

Meanwhile Nan meets and finally is courted by George Gerry. One of the more interesting episodes in their courtship occurs when they are walking in the country and encounter a man with a dislocated shoulder. Nan deftly takes charge and quickly resets the shoulder. All are amazed that a woman should have such skill, but George is threatened and begins to resent her assertive behavior.

The courtship finally terminates in her rejecting George's offer of marriage. She has found that she cannot play the role of "yielding maiden," and that life as a wife would be unbearably confining for her:

It is not my whole self longing for his love and companionship. If I heard he had gone to the other side of the world for years and years, I should be glad and not sorry. I know that all the world's sympathy and all tradition fight on his side; but I can look forward and see something a thousand times better than being his wife, and living here in Dunport keeping his house, and trying to forget all that nature fitted me to do.

Thus, her decision, like that of several previous Jewett characters, is basically a choice between the confining life of a small town, to which is now associated the traditional role of woman, and an expansive, exciting self-directed professional life.

That Nan eventually returns to her own region to practice suggests that like her author she has discovered a way to combine rural life with intellectual and moral fulfillment. The last words of the novel occur as Nan is wandering in the country: "Suddenly she reached her hands upward in an ecstasy of life and strength and gladness. 'O God,' she said, 'I thank thee for my future.' "

The culmination of this period of Jewett's work comes with "A White Heron." Here the themes of country versus city, pastoral versus industrial, and female versus male are woven together in what has proven to be Jewett's most popular story. It has been reprinted in numerous collections, translated into several languages, including Japanese, and has recently been made into a beautiful film by Jane Morrison.[5]

The story is set deep in the Maine woods and concerns a confrontation between an urban visitor, an ornithologist, and Sylvia, another of Jewett's young untamed rural girls. Sylvia lives with her grandmother. The confrontation is over a white heron that the young man wishes to kill and stuff for his collection. Sylvia knows where the bird is and is tempted to reveal its whereabouts to the young man, but finally remains loyal to her forest companion and refuses to disclose its location.

From the beginning of the story we find Sylvia happy in her rural setting. Her name has obvious pastoral connotations. She feels "a part of the gray shadows and the moving leaves." In contrast to this contentment is the "crowded manufacturing town" where she used to live. There a "great red-faced boy . . . used to chase and frighten her." When she first hears the ornithologist's whistle she is "horror-stricken." It is "not a bird's whistle, which would have a sort of friendliness, but a boy's whistle, determined, and somewhat aggressive." He is immediately perceived as "the enemy."

Sylvia's defenses weaken somewhat as the visitor's stay continues. The suggestion of a potential romance repeats the suitor pattern we have seen in earlier Jewett works. Once again the suitor is rejected in favor of a higher good: in this case that good is the preservation of the sanctity of the natural world against the destructive intrusion of this urban stranger.

On their rambles through the forest it is "the young man going first and Sylvia following. . . . She did not lead the guest, she only followed, and there was no such thing as speaking first." As in earlier stories, there are allusions to the restrictions on the female role. Sylvia is attracted to the young man at least in part because he represents knowledge and excitement beyond her limited rural range. The author comments on how strong a motivation this is for her to betray the bird's whereabouts.

Alas, if the great wave of human interest which flooded for the first time this dull little life should sweep away the satisfactions of an existence heart to heart with nature and the dumb life of the forest!

But Sylvia finds that she is able to expand her horizons by herself. In climbing a tall tree early one morning to seek out the bird's location she sees things she had never seen before: the ocean, ships at sail and finally the white heron itself. This knowledge strengthens her will and reinforces her solidarity with nature and her peaceful sanctuary.

The murmur of the pine's green branches is in her ears, she remembers how the white heron came flying through the golden air and how they watched the sea and the morning together, and Sylvia cannot speak; she cannot tell the heron's secret and give its life away.

Despite the extraordinary emotional power of this story, it suffers somewhat from the distance between the author and the girl. Sylvia never seems to understand entirely why she acts the way she does. Indeed, we learn at the end of the story that she regrets the loss of the ornithologist's friendship caused by her decision. She has even forgotten

her sorrow at the sharp report of his gun and the piteous sight of thrushes and sparrows dropping silent to the ground, their songs hushed and their pretty feathers stained and wet with blood.

Yet it is evident from the fact that Jewett chooses to end the story with this gruesome image that the author is quite clear why the girl chose the way she did. Within Jewett's own value-world, indeed, it is inconceivable that she could have chosen otherwise. The girl's dumb incomprehension of her actions is not characteristic of Jewett's female characters, who as we have seen, are usually acutely rational and articulate. Probably Jewett has attempted to fashion a preliterate country child, someone alien to her own experience. For me Sylvia is not quite believable.

Nevertheless the tensions and conflicts expressed in the story are quite believable. It remains one of Jewett's most successful attempts at dramatic confrontation. As Annis Pratt has pointed out, "A White Heron" is really an ironic version of the traditional fairy tale in which the handsome prince awakens the sleeping beauty. Here the prince only initiates the awakening; the main awakening is accomplished by the girl herself, and the prince is ultimately rejected. Pratt comments,

one suspects that if Sylvia had been the princess of the fairy tale in which a toad turned into a handsome prince, she would have been disappointed, preferring the toad.[6]

Like *A Country Doctor* and to some extent *A Marsh Island,* "A White Heron" resolves the conflict between urban and rural by affirming the values of country life and rejecting the evils of the industrial city (symbolized in the man's gun), while at the same time acknowledging the limitations of the country world and recognizing the excitement and opportunity for growth the city represents. That Sylvia, like Nan in *A Country Doctor* and Dick in *A Marsh Island,* is able to synthesize the best of both worlds is a reflection of Jewett's own successful resolution of this dilemma at this period in her development.

4

Isolation versus Community: 1886–1895

Yankee individualism, its virtues and its shortcomings, has always attracted New England writers. Sarah Orne Jewett was drawn to the topic during her third decade of literary production. She seemed concerned to portray the evils of extreme individualism and to promote the virtues of association. While she continued to write stories of resourceful, independent spinsters, they became less numerous. Instead there is an increasing concentration of stories that focus on individuals moving out of their shells of isolation toward participation in a larger community.

Two stories present examples of New England self-reliant individualism gone amok. "The King of Folly Island" and "The Landscape Chamber" depict selfish tyrants who, out of spite, have chosen lives of permanent exile. Several other stories, however, present characters who attempt to move beyond the barriers of ego and to establish community. In nearly all cases it is men who are the egotistical isolates and women who create and sustain the communal experience. A considerable number of these women choose to bond primarily with one another.

The works that fall within this period are *The King of Folly Island and Other People* (1888), *Strangers and Wayfarers* (1890), *A Native of Winby and Other Tales* (1893), and *The Life of Nancy* (1895). In addition, in 1890 Houghton Mifflin published a selection of eight stories reprinted from previous volumes entitled *Tales of New England*. Jewett also wrote three works for juveniles during this period. The first of these was *The Story of the Normans, Told Chiefly in Relation to Their Conquest of England* (1887), an inferior work that mixed history and myth indiscriminately and allowed its author to indulge in one of her few pet prejudices, the notion that the Normans (from whom she believed herself descended) were a favored race whose contribution to English culture redeemed it from semibarbarism. The other two works for adolescents were *Betty Leicester, A Story For Girls* (1890), considered a children's classic in the nineteenth century, and *Betty Leicester's English Xmas, A New Chapter of An Old Story* (1894). These portray the development through adolescence of one of Jewett's characteristically assertive female characters. Jewett's moral here is also characteristic: one must develop a sense of self-reliance and not depend on others to make one's way.

[Betty] was eager, as all girls are, for one single controlling fate or fortune to call out all her growing energies, but she was aware . . . that she herself must choose and provide; she must learn to throw herself heartily into her life just as it was.

That Jewett enjoins such a philosophy on her female readers is another instance of her personal advocacy of a kind of individualistic feminism.

The majority of the works of this period suggest, however, that a simpleminded assertion of individualism is not enough. Jewett seems to have been moving toward a more complex moral and philosophical statement about life and of the importance of the social bond. This was to culminate in her masterpiece *The Country of the Pointed Firs*, which is discussed in the next chapter. Undoubtedly it also reflects Jewett's growing personal awareness of how central her own community of friends had become in providing her with support and with what she called "transcendence."

"A Garden Story" (*The Independent* 22 July 1886, *Uncollected Stories* 1971) is the first story in this period to present a spinster who chooses to give up a solitary existence in favor of sharing her home with another woman. Miss Ann Dunning, an ardent gardener, has a characteristically suspicious attitude toward men, especially since one ruined her garden by pulling up half of her good plants along with the weeds. "She would not have a man about that part of her small domain—not she!" She is lonely, however, and decides to participate in a summer program whereby city orphans are brought to country homes for a week. Peggy McAllister proves to be a pathetic and appealing waif who identifies with the weeds and thinnings in the garden and insists on saving the latter to send to friends in a Boston hospital. Ann finally adopts her permanently.

Another story about a summer exchange program is "Miss Esther's Guest" (*A Native of Winby* 1893), one of Jewett's most delightful tales. Miss Esther Porley, left alone after mother's death, decides to take in a boarder under the "Country Week" fresh air program. Since this program generally brings mothers and children to the country, Miss Esther is surprised when her guest turns out to be an elderly gentleman, Mr. Rill, who descends from the train with his bird cage and carpetbag. They get on very well, however; he extends his stay a month, and eventually they decide, as Esther puts it, to "take the step."

Most of the stories in *The King of Folly Island* deal directly with the theme of isolation versus community. The title story (*Harper's Magazine* December 1886, *The King of Folly Island* 1888) is about George Quint who, out of dislike for his neighbors, has exiled himself, his wife, and his daughter on a remote island for over a quarter of a century. Jewett gave the setting an allegorical name, Folly Island.

Quint has established a virtual tyranny over the women, who long for human companionship. The protagonist-visitor, a businessman (through whose eyes the story is told) points out that the burden of exile is greatest on the women because, while George continues to meet his friends when out fishing, they are confined to the island. "There was no actual exile in the fisherman's lot after all; he met his old acquaintances almost daily on the fishing grounds, and it was upon the women of the household that an unmistakeable burden of isolation had fallen."

After many years the wife dies, apparently of emotional starvation. George commented of his wife: "She never fought me, . . . but it aged her, fetchin' of her away from all her folks, an' out of where she was wonted." Phebe, the daughter, has developed what appears to be consumption (tuberculosis). The visitor suggests that she ought to be hospitalized on the mainland, but George refuses to go: "my vow is my vow." The visitor realizes that Quint's stand is "willful" and "selfish." "Was it possible that Quint was a tyrant, and had never let this grown woman leave his chosen isle? Freedom indeed!" Eventually Phebe also dies.

In one of the more pathetic scenes in the story, Phebe is so eager to participate in social affairs that she watches a funeral procession on a neighboring island through a spyglass. The visitor comments once again on the deprivation that has been forced upon the women: "The tough fisherman, with his pet doctrines and angry aversions, could have no idea of the loneliness of his wife and daughter all these unvarying years on his Folly Island."

This story is archetypal. It seems to be Jewett's comment on the patriarchal tyranny of the nuclear family of Victorian America. If so, it is a social pattern she emphatically rejects. A similar situation was described in equally negative terms in a story published nearly a year later, "The Landscape Chamber" (*Atlantic Monthly* November 1887, *The King of Folly Island* 1888).

Here the tyrant is once again a patriarch and the tyrannized a woman, his daughter. In this case the narrator is clearly a persona for Jewett: a vigorous horsewoman off on a horseback excursion by herself, carrying a much-loved copy of *A Sentimental Journey*. As in earlier stories, this figure is a strong, free-willed woman, the antithesis of the weak-kneed invalid we have come to associate with Victorian womanhood. Also as in similar stories such as "An October Ride," the horsewoman character is subjected to hostile stares (in the earlier story little boys had thrown stones at her and her horse) and suspicious innkeepers. Evidently such expeditions by unaccompanied young women were socially taboo.

On this ride she happens upon a rundown decrepit farm where she asks to spend the night, as her horse has developed shoe trouble. Here live this strange couple. The father is supposedly the victim of an inherited mental disease of "monomania," which he uses to account for his extreme behavior, his utter miserliness and total withdrawal from society. There is a Calvinistic doom about the situation that the optimistic young narrator rejects. "What power could burst the bonds, and liberate the man and woman ... from a mysterious tyranny?" she wonders.

The daughter is particularly pathetic. "You surely have friends?" The narrator asks her.

"Only at a distance," said she, sadly. "I fear that they are
no longer friends. I have *you*," she added, turning to me
quickly, in a pathetic way that made me wish to put my
arms about her. "I have been longing for a friendly face.
Yes, it is very hard," and she drearily went out of the
door . . . .

In the end the narrator cannot accept this supposedly predestined tyranny. "Among human be-
ings," she declares, "there is freedom. . . . We can
climb to our best possibilities, and outgrow our worst
inheritance." The novelty of Jewett's position here,
as elsewhere, is that she continually applies this doctrine of American optimism to women.

In the final arrangement of stories in *The King
of Folly Island* a joyous tale of celebration and community is placed between the two grim stories just
discussed. This is "The Courting of Sister Wisby,"
(*Atlantic Monthly* May 1887, *The King of Folly Island*
1888), certainly one of Jewett's masterpieces.

In this story Jewett used her characteristic
tale-within-a-tale format. The difference this time is
that the frame plot, that which describes the relationship between the narrator and the people she
encounters, holds equal weight with the interior, or
narrated, tale. This important structural development prefigures the unique form she was to devise
for *The Country of the Pointed Firs,* but which she has
used from her earliest stories, if sometimes less skill-
fully.

The story begins, as do so many Jewett stories,
with the narrator-persona wandering in the country
on a late New England summer day. She encounters
Mrs. Goodsoe, an herb gatherer, and one of Jewett's
most memorable creations. Mrs. Goodsoe is collect-
ing "mulleins." The narrator volunteers help and
the two engage in lengthy and animated conversa-

tion. This scene stands in high contrast to the miserable isolation depicted in the surrounding stories.

Mrs. Goodsoe is a woman of decided opinions and belongs to that Jewett breed of women that has deep reservations about technological "progress," especially, in this case, modern medicine. City peoples' ill health is due to their lack of knowledge of herb medicine. She castigates young doctors who though they be "bilin' over with book-larnin' . . . is truly ignorant of what to do for the sick. . . . Book-fools I call 'em. . . ." She hearkens back to the matrilineal tradition of women healers, such as her own mother, who had an extensive knowledge of curative herbs and from whom Mrs. Goodsoe learned her trade.

Her mother was an environmental purist. Herbs should never be imported. Rather "folks was meant to be doctored with the stuff that grew right about 'em; 't was sufficient, an' so ordered." Mrs. Goodsoe also distrusts modern rapid transportation. She warns that there is sure to be "some sort of a set-back one o' these days." People were not meant to travel all over the place. "In old times . . . they stood in their lot an' place, and weren't all just alike, either, same as pine-spills." The narrator suggests lamely that modern travel has provided people with new opportunities for enrichment. But her interlocutor silently demurs.

Mrs. Goodsoe begins reminiscing about neighbors, in particular Deacon Brimblecom. Thus begins the central tale. Brimblecom was a kind of revivalist preacher who got it in his head that he had been called by a "spirit bride" to "dwell among the angels while yet on airth." So he left his wife and four children, but "by an' by the spirit bride didn't turn out to be much of a housekeeper, an' he had always been used to good livin', so he sneaked home

ag'in." Eventually his wife died, and he met Eliza
Wisby.

"The way he came a-courtin' o' Sister Wisby was
this: she went a-courtin' o' him." Sister Wisby was
prominent in the revivalist sect herself. Both were
great at "bawling" in meeting. Sister Wisby decided
that it would be sensible if they were to live together
before engaging in a more serious commitment,
since "so much harm come from hasty unions." So,
one day the neighbors saw the deacon go riding
down to her house with "a gre't coopful of hens" on
the wagon. Come spring, they saw him riding back.
She had kicked him out. Later, however, she re-
called him when she remembered that he owed her
labor for the winter's lodging. This time things went
better and they married. But in her will Sister Wisby
left everything to his daughter Phebe. (This is another suggestion of matrilineality, an interest that
becomes pronounced in later Jewett works.)

Bonding between women continues as an important theme in several succeeding stories. Three
of these concern the resolution of ancient feuds
through the efforts of the women involved. "Law
Lane" (*Scribner's Magazine* December 1887, *The King
of Folly Island* 1888) follows a format similar to "The
Courting of Sister Wisby." Mrs. Powder goes out
"blueberrying" with Lyddy Bangs. Their conversation turns to the feud between the Crosbys and the
Barnets, who have been disputing a strip of land
between their properties for generations.

A Romeo and Juliet situation has developed,
however; Ezra Barnet and Ruth Crosby have fallen
in love and wish to marry. Mrs. Barnet, the family
matriarch, falls ill, and is convinced by Mrs. Powder,
who is nursing her, to bless the marriage on what
appears to be her death bed. She recovers, however,
and suspects she has been had by Mrs. Powder. But
no mind, the feud has been ended, and on Christmas

Day. Here again we see women's efforts succeeding in repairing ancient egotistical antagonisms and creating new bonds of community. The Christian association with community had been drawn in an earlier story, "A Christmas Guest" [*Wide Awake* January 1887] in which a young girl, alone on Christmas Eve tending her sick grandmother, is mysteriously visited in the midst of a winter storm by a stranger who brings her comradeship and thus eases her anxiety.

"Fair Day" (*Scribner's Magazine* August 1888, *Strangers and Wayfarers* 1890) also deals with the termination of a lengthy feud. In this case it has been between sisters-in-law Mercy Bascom, a Civil War widow who had raised four children, and Ruth Bascom, also a war widow with several offspring. They decide to reconcile on the day of the local fair, making it a "fair day" in more ways than one.

"Dan's Wife" (*Harper's Bazar* 2 August 1889) is a story with an interesting publishing history. Lost for nearly ninety years, it was only rediscovered in 1976.[1] It too deals with two women in-laws who manage to overcome a territorial clash and live together harmoniously. Ann Parish, the central character, is a proud matriarch, somewhat of a female analogue to George Quint and the father in "The Landscape Chamber." She is proud of her ancestry and her meticulous housekeeping and ambitious to see her children succeed. She has already driven her daughter Eliza to an early grave by forcing her to attend a high-pressure school. This proved to be too much for the sensitive child, who died of consumption. As the story opens Ann is waiting in her home to welcome her son Dan and his new bride Hannah, who are moving in.

The two women do not hit it off, although Hannah is eager to please and understands that she is intruding into the older woman's domain. But Ann begins nagging Hannah over her allegedly laggard housework and correcting her pronunciation of words. The pressure affects Hannah, who like Eliza becomes seriously ill. This serves to awaken Ann to her behavior, however. She repents as Hannah recovers and treats her henceforth as a daughter. Thus the tyrannical figure relents and social harmony results.

A story similar in theme but with the novelty of a French Canadian setting is "Mère Pochette" (*Harper's Magazine* March 1888, *The King of Folly Island* 1888). Here the clash is between a strong-willed grandmother and her granddaughter, Manon, who is named for her. Mère Pochette's daughter and son-in-law have died, leaving her to bring up Manon. Like Ann Parish, Mère Pochette is tyrannical and dictatorial. Manon falls in love with Charles Pictou, an unambitious local boy. The grandmother opposes the match. Charles goes to the United States to make his fortune and prove himself, but Mère Pochette destroys all his letters home to his lover. Manon rapidly fades away until, when she is near death, the grandmother repents. Charles returns, they marry, and harmony is restored. Jewett completed one other story with a French Canadian setting during this period, "Little French Mary" (*Philadelphia Press* 2 June 1895, *The Life of Nancy* 1895).

Several other stories written during this period present women working together or helping one another. One of the most anthologized of Jewett's stories, "Miss Tempy's Watchers" (*Atlantic Monthly* March 1888, *The King of Folly Island* 1888), is among these. In this story two old schoolmates, one wealthy and the other poor, have been called upon to wake their old friend Temperance Dent. It is suggested that before her death Temperance had chosen them for this task in "some hope that they might become closer friends in this period of intimate partnership, and that the richer woman might better understand the burdens of the poorer."

In the course of the evening Mrs. Crowe, the wealthier woman, begins to eulogize their fallen friend, noting especially her generosity. Sarah Ann Binson, the poorer woman, who has the burden of supporting "an inefficient widowed sister and six unpromising and unwilling nieces and nephews," listens silently. Mrs. Crowe begins to apply the model of Miss Tempy to herself, resolving to become more charitable in the future.

Meanwhile we learn more about Miss Tempy and her almost psychic sensitivity to others. Sarah Ann exclaims at one point, "Oh, dear me, how I shall miss talkin' over things with her! She always sensed things, and got just the p'int you meant." Tempy had a way of communicating with the natural world as well. "She'd go out in the spring and tend to [her old quince tree] and look at it so pleasant, and kind of expect the old thorny thing into bloomin'." Sarah Ann notes that Tempy had the same effect on people. As the hours pass, it becomes apparent that her spiritual presence is having such an effect on the two watchers: urging them to bloom with charity for each other. Finally the women drowse. "Sister Binson closed her eyes first . . . and Mrs. Crowe glanced at her compassionately, with a new sympathy for the hard-worked little woman." It seems that Tempy's hope has been realized, that the two women have been drawn together at her wake.

In her study *Communities of Women,* Nina Auerbach sees this story as an archetypal example of a community of women. Brought together momentarily "at the margins of the social and natural world," they achieve "an almost magical af-

finity with the sources of transformation and re-
birth." A "miraculous sisterhood" has been
formed.[2]

Another story that deals with what is at least a
potential wake is "The Passing of Sister Barsett"
(*Cosmopolitan* May 1892, *A Native of Winby* 1893).
The story presents another strong image of sisterhood, this time in a more humorous vein. Miss Sarah
Ellen Dow comes to visit Mercy Crane, a widow, after
having tended Sister Barsett in what she thinks have
been her last hours. They discuss the virtues and
weaknesses of the deceased and lament the vultur-
ous behavior of her two sisters. Sarah and Mercy also
reassure one another that when their time comes,
they will tend each other. After tea another neighbor comes by and exclaims that Sister Barsett is
clamoring for Sarah to return. Apparently she had
not died but had gone into a relapse. Sarah hurries
back, and Mercy laughs to herself long after Sarah is
out of sight.

"The Guests of Mrs. Timms" (*Century Magazine*
February 1894, *The Life of Nancy* 1895) is another
comic tale about women socializing, this time not too
successfully. Mrs. Persis Flagg, a widow, and Miss
Esther Pickett decide one day to take the stage to pay
a surprise visit to their old friend Mrs. Timms. In the
stagecoach they meet another woman, who is going
to visit Mrs. Brackett, a woman she had met some
time before at a conference. This visit, too, is unan-
nounced. A suspenseful drama develops when the
woman descends the stage at Mrs. Brackett's and her
trunk is unloaded. Mrs. Brackett looks dumb-
founded; she barely remembers this person, who
has obviously arrived for a lengthy stay. As the stage
leaves, it seems likely the visitor will be mounting it
again that evening for the return run.

Mrs. Timms, however, seems equally uncomfortable about the arrival of her guests. She receives

them somewhat coldly, does not ask them to remove their hats, and keeps them in the parlor. Despite their long trip, they leave her shortly to visit another old friend, who greets them warmly and feeds them. But it is they who are on the return stage that evening and not the guest of Mrs. Brackett.

Another, more serious story continues the theme of sisterhood, once again with the well-off taking charitable responsibility for the poor. "The Town Poor" (*Atlantic Monthly* July 1890, *Strangers and Wayfarers* 1890) also opens with a visit being made by two women, Mrs. William Trimble and Miss Rebecca Wright. They are going to see "the town poor," Ann and Mandanna Bray, who are kept by the James family. Under the welfare system practiced in this town (and presumably throughout rural New England), when people became destitute, others in the town would bid on the cost of their welfare. The low bidder was awarded their charge by the town, which then paid him or her the welfare costs. The poor were thus farmed out, so to speak, to live with the lowest bidder. The possibilities for fraud under this system are obvious, and in the case of the Bray sisters the James family had apparently been pocketing the welfare payments they had been receiving from the town. The sisters had therefore been reduced to shockingly wretched conditions. When the two visitors discover this, they vow to force the town selectmen to put up enough money to maintain the sisters at their own home in town, which they had been forced to give up earlier.

One of the most memorable of the group of stories that deals with female bonding is "In Dark New England Days" (*Century Magazine* October 1890, *Strangers and Wayfarers* 1890). As in "Miss Tempy's Watchers," the women seem to have a connection to the supernatural; however, in this case it is not of benign magic but witchcraft. We also see in this story the pattern of the tyrannical patriarch browbeating the women of the family. But here the women take their revenge.

The Knowles daughters Hannah and Betsey have been "slaves" to their father, an old sea captain, for decades, until his death. The story opens with his funeral. At last they are free. That evening they open the old sea chest that is their inheritance and discover a hoard of gold coins—at last, some reward for their years of forced labor. Unfortunately, however, a prowler has been watching them at the window, and while they sleep, steals the money. The women, wildly disappointed, accuse a neighbor, Enoch Holt, of the crime, but he is tried and acquitted. After the hearing Hannah accuses him to his face. He swears his innocence, raising his right hand. Hannah curses the hand.

As time passes three members of the Holt family, including Enoch, lose the use of their right hand. The sisters become more and more witchlike. Neighbors begin exchanging stories they have heard about witchcraft, including tales about voodoo practiced on remote islands where natives cast spells on one another with curses. The sisters have turned to psychic vengeance for their years of oppression and abuse and for their final bitter disappointment.

Another story written during this period in which the intransigence of a willful family patriarch leads to disaster is "A Neighbor's Landmark" (*Century Magazine* December 1894, *The Life of Nancy* 1894). John Packer, tyrannical and contrary, makes a deal with a greedy capitalist named Ferris to sell two giant pines on his property for seventy-five dollars. His wife, daughter, and neighbors all oppose this, because the trees are familiar landmarks that have become part of their lives. Finally Packer relents at the last minute and the trees are saved. One of Jewett's most biting attacks on capitalistic spoilage of rural landscapes occurs in this story. Ferris has exploited many a farmer.

He . . . had taken advantage of the hard times, and of more than one man's distress, to buy woodland at far less than its value. More than that, he always stripped land to the bare skin . . . he left nothing to grow; no sapling-oak or pine stood where his hand had been.

Jewett had delivered equally harsh words in a sketch published a few years earlier, "The White Rose Road" (*Atlantic Monthly* September 1889, *Strangers and Wayfarers* 1890). Here she decried the pollution of the Piscataqua River near South Berwick by factories and sawmills. The salmon, once abundant, were nearly gone. "I think the need of preaching against this bad economy is very great," she wrote. "Man has done his best to ruin the world he lives in."

Through the decade 1886 to 1895, Jewett also produced a set of stories about single women. Nearly all of these, however, unlike her earlier stories about spinsters, portray women victimized by men. The men in these stories are not malicious tyrants like those discussed above but are simply insensitive, weak and incompetent.

"Miss Peck's Promotion" (*Scribner's Magazine* June 1887, *The King of Folly Island* 1888) is similar to "Miss Manning's Minister," discussed previously, and to "A Second Spring," discussed below. In all three, a recently widowed man calls upon a neighboring woman to serve as his temporary housekeeper until he gets back on his feet. In two of the stories the woman is rewarded for her service by an offer of marriage. But Eliza Peck is used and discarded.

After the wife of Mr. Elbury, the minister, dies, Eliza goes to care for him. Her main interest in him is that "he stood . . . for a widened life, . . . a larger circle of human interests; in fact, his existence had made all the difference between her limited rural home and that connection with the great world which even the most contracted parsonage is sure to hold." "She liked the new excitement and authority, and grew more and more happy in the exercise of powers which solitary life at the farm would hardly arouse or engage." Mr. Elbury thus represents for her a chance both to deepen her social involvement and to develop her own potential. He offers an escape from rural isolation and boredom.

Her friends warn her, however, that she is too good for him. And indeed he proves himself to be an ingrate and a fool by marrying a young, vapid, helpless creature. To add insult to injury, he asks Eliza to stay on as housekeeper. But she returns to her farm, leaving the couple in their helplessness; her pride remains intact, and she comes to see the virtues of her old rural life and vows to continue taking care of others.

A similar story is "A Village Shop" (*The King of Folly Island* 1888), one of Jewett's lesser-known feminist classics. In this story Miss Esther Jaffrey sacrifices herself to support her brother Leonard, who is the last and the least of the Jaffreys. "If she had been the son how she could work and win her way, and not be the least of those who had borne the Jaffrey name. . . . But she was only a woman . . . ." Leonard even quits school and returns home, a parasite. The family fortune has been used up, and Esther has to open a shop to support the two of them. Leonard continues to sit around "with as much energy as a barnacle." Esther "would have found it convenient if Leonard could have bestirred his feeble muscles enough to drive a nail straight or grapple with a rusty screw, but she never reproached him and learned to use a hammer herself instead."

Finally a wealthy townsman asks the Jaffreys to tutor his daughter Nelly. Leonard falls in love with her, much to Esther's dismay. After all her efforts to remain financially independent, Leonard's forthcoming marriage will make them depend on John Gaunt, Nelly's father. Moreover, Esther resents the fact that while she has sacrificed so much for him, in the end he receives the ultimate reward, love, and she receives nothing. The injustice of her situation is nearly unbearable to her. At the last moment, Leonard, who had been a haphazard scholar, is named town librarian. With his new income he offers to support Esther and suggests that she give up her shop. "Never!" is her proud response.

Another independent woman is portrayed in "The Growtown 'Bugle' " (*Harper's Weekly* 18 August 1888, *Uncollected Stories* 1971). This moralistic story preaches once again the evils of greed and the virtues of charity, but in the course develops an O. Henry situation in which a spinster makes a fortune speculating by mail. Miss Prudence Fellows of New England happens to notice a newspaper advertisement about real estate investment opportunities in Growtown, Kansas. While the scheme sounds patently fraudulent, she manages to come out on top, eventually reaping a considerable profit. She fails, however, to use her money charitably, and as a result remains poor in spirit.

"Going to Shrewsbury" (*Atlantic Monthly* July 1889, *Strangers and Wayfarers* 1890), also about a single woman, is considerably different in tone. This is a simple but moving story about the uprooting of an aged woman late in life. The narrator meets Mrs.

Peat on the train going to Shrewsbury where she is to resettle with nieces. Mrs. Peat has been cheated out of her farm by a relative, Isaiah Peat, and has been left destitute and homeless. The narrator learns later that while Mrs. Peat seemed to be happy in Shrewsbury and was well treated by her nieces, she died within the year.

Another story that shows a woman victimized by a shiftless male, but that has a happy ending, is "Jim's Little Woman" (*Harper's Magazine* December 1890, *A Native of Winby* 1893). In the vein of the sentimental novel this story depicts the long-suffering wife of an alcoholic but well-meaning sailor. One day his ship returns home without him aboard, and his mates say he had died in a foreign port. His wife never gives up hope, however, and eventually he does return, prosperous and re-formed. The story is set in St. Augustine, Florida, where Jewett had vacationed. The locale is richly described. The style in this story is also noteworthy. It is unusually objective and distanced from the subjects, and anticipates in tone the style of Willa Cather.

One further story in this set that deals with essentially solitary figures is "The Failure of David Berry" (*Harper's Magazine* June 1891, *A Native of Winby* 1893). This piece is somewhat atypical, for the protagonist is a man and his failure is unmitigated. It is typical of Jewett, however, in that it portrays sympathetically a small artisan who is gradually being displaced by mass production. David Berry is a shoemaker. His business declines as cheaper "ready-made" shoes become popular. He gradually goes into debt; his shop is repossessed and he finally dies of a broken heart. His wife has to auction off their personal possessions in order to eke out a living in her later years. Characteristically, Jewett does not

take the political stand against industrial capitalism
that would seem to be occasioned by this pathetic
situation; rather she sees the personal greed of the
person to whom Berry is in debt as the cause of the
tragedy. Here as elsewhere, Jewett does not express
a comprehensive political viewpoint. She attributes
evil to the vices of individuals rather than systems.

While these stories focus upon the individual
primarily in isolation, another set of stories written
during this period dwells more on people in community with one another, thus bringing into relief
another aspect of the isolation versus community
theme. Most of these concern late-in-life romances
that bring long-isolated people together. Typical of
this genre is "Told in the Tavern" (*New York World*
15 April 1894, *Uncollected Stories* 1971). In this piece
a stranger comes to town and sees his own name on a
tombstone. He is Perkins, who had left town thirty
years before to make his fortune in the West. He
learns in the tavern that a lonely spinster, Miss Abby
Sands, had set up the tombstone for her lover years
before. He announces that he is that lover and is
about to return to her. Needless to say, the tavern
guests are speechless.

Another story of a native's return is "A Native of
Winby" (*Atlantic Monthly* May 1891, *A Native of Winby*
1893). The Honorable Joe Langway, a local boy who
had become a general in the Civil War and later a
United States senator, returns to his birthplace
Winby. One episode that occurs during his visit
home is an encounter with Abby Harran Hender,
with whom he had had a youthful romance. They
rekindle some of the old feeling.

"A Winter Courtship" (*Atlantic Monthly*
February 1889, *Strangers and Wayfarers* 1890) is an
amusing tale about another late-in-life romance.
Mr. Jefferson Briley, a stage driver, and his pas-

senger, elderly Mrs. Fanny Tobin, get to talking
during a seven-mile trip. They consider their common lot—both are widowed. He proposes; she ac-
cepts. The abruptness of the courtship is due to the
practical calculations each in turn makes mentally of
the advantages living together would bring.

"A Second Spring" (*Harper's Magazine*
December 1893, *The Life of Nancy* 1895) also deals
with a practical marriage arrangement, but in a
slightly more serious vein. Israel Haydon, a sixty-
eight-year-old farmer, has just lost his wife. He is
desolate; his house falls into disrepair. Neighbor
women comment to one another: "Men is boys . . .
the more you treat 'em like boys, the better they
think you use 'em. They always want motherin' an'
somebody to come to." Finally Maria Davenport is
hired as a housekeeper. She gets things back in
order, but then people start gossiping about their
living together unmarried. So when she threatens to
leave, he proposes. Thus begins his "second spring."

"All My Sad Captains" (*Century Magazine*
September 1895, *The Life of Nancy* 1895) is likewise a
story of autumn courtship. In this case three retired
sea captains court a widow, Mrs. Maria Lunn. Two
of them see the arrangement as a business deal, but
she chooses Captain Witherspoon, the man who
genuinely cares for her. This plot had been brought
to perfection earlier by Jewett in her classic "The
Only Rose" (*Atlantic Monthly* January 1894, *The Life
of Nancy* 1895).

In "The Only Rose," the decision is not over
which suitor the heroine should choose but which of
her three dead husbands to honor with the finest
rose in her collection. Mrs. Bickford deliberates at
great length, considering the virtues and shortcomings of each of her fallen mates. Mr. Bickford had
left her financially secure, for which she was grate-

ful; Mr. Wallis was handsome and an animated con-
versationalist ("splendid company for winter evenings"), but unsuccessful in business; Albert Fraley
was her first love. Her heart still belongs to him. " 'I
expect 't was what they call fallin' in love,' she added,
in a different tone; 'he wa'n't nothin' but a boy, an' I
wa'n't nothin' but a girl, but we was dreadful
happy.' " Still Mrs. Bickford cannot bring herself to
place the rose on the grave of one to the exclusion of
the others. She asks her nephew to place the flowers
on the graves for her. When he returns, he tells her
he kept the perfect rose for himself and his fiancée.
This is fitting, for the nephew has reminded her all
along of Albert. " 'My first husband was just such a
tall, straight young man as you be,' she said as they
drove along. 'The flower he first give me was a
rose.' " As in all her best pieces, Jewett managed in
this story to combine sentiment with comic irony,
keeping both in delicate balance.

The story that culminates the examination of
the theme of isolation versus community is "The
Flight of Betsey Lane," (*Scribner's Magazine* August
1893, *A Native of Winby* 1893). Betsey Lane is a
member of the Byfleet Poor-house community of
women, and is close friends with two other residents,
Aunt Lavinia Dow, who suffers from rheumatism,
and Miss Peggy Bond, who is severely "upsighted."
Betsey Lane at sixty-nine is the youngest of the
group. One day her former employer comes to visit
Betsey and leaves her a considerable sum of money.
Soon after this, Betsey disappears from the
poorhouse farm. All fear the worst. However, Betsey had merely decided to assert her independence
and fulfill a secret wish, to attend the Centennial
celebration in Philadelphia. It was 1876. Betsey hops
a train, proceeds to the festival, marvels at all the
new inventions, buys gifts for her friends, and

finally returns home to spend her last years with her
own community of friends. Betsey Lane is a model
of one who manages to synthesize her need for independence and her need for community, and in
this sense provides a fitting resolution to the concern that so dominates this decade of Jewett's writing.

During this period Jewett also experimented
with three groups of stories set outside her usual
New England locale and dealing with themes she did
not usually handle. The first of these groups was set
in the South or dealt with the Civil War; the second
was set in Ireland and concerned Irish immigrants;
the third dealt with French Canadians. In all these
she effectively created dialect appropriate to the
respective culture. It seems likely that her purpose
in exploring cultures remote to her and her readers
was to counter popular prejudices. In her second
preface to *Deephaven,* published in 1893, she cited a
"noble saying of Plato" that "the best thing that can
be done for the people of a state is to make them
acquainted with one another." This she claims to
have been part of her motivation for *Deephaven* but it
applies to the stories under consideration here as
well. For southern whites, Irish Catholics and
French Canadians were hardly popular groups with
Jewett's Yankee readership in the 1890s.

Two of the war-related stories are set in the
South, and two concern northern veterans who reminisce about Civil War experiences. "The Mistress of
Sydenham Plantation" (*Atlantic Monthly* August
1888, *Strangers and Wayfarers* 1890) deals with the
pathos of the postwar desolation in the South. It
appears to be set in the Tidewater area of Maryland
and portrays a deranged elderly white woman who
decides to return to her plantation twenty years
after the war. Her servant, Peter, a former slave who

has remained with her, warns her not to make the trip. He knows but does not tell her that her former home had been burned to the ground years before, and the plantation subdivided among the former slaves. Despite the warning she returns, accompanied by the old servant, and finds that only the chimney remains standing. On the way they encounter an elderly black woman who is just as confused mentally as her former mistress. On the next day, which is Easter, Peter helps her to church. The point of the story seems to be that nobody benefited from the destruction of the South.

A story that is even more sympathetic to the ruined Southern aristocrats is "A War Debt" (*Harper's Magazine* January 1895, *The Life of Nancy* 1895). This story is one of Jewett's few but unfortunate lapses. It is blatantly racist, both in promoting the Normans once again and in condemning the free slaves for their allegedly irresponsible behavior. In the story, Tom Burton, a Bostonian, is charged by his grandmother to return a silver cup her son had stolen from a plantation during the war. Tom goes to Virginia, sees stereotypically shiftless blacks in way stations, and finds the old plantation owner Bellamy still taking care of those who had chosen to remain with him. In the train station he notices a white woman who seems to be of Norman ancestry. She is one of the aristocratic Bellamys of the plantation he is visiting, and he later courts her. Fortunately, Jewett only wrote one story of this type.

"Decoration Day" (*Harper's Magazine* June 1892, *A Native of Winby* 1893) concerns several Civil War veterans who decide to hold a parade on Decoration Day (now Memorial Day) to attempt to revive public spirit in Barlow. It is ironic that the story suggests that since the veterans are dying out, such ceremonies will soon be history. "Peach-tree Joe"

(*The Californian Illustrated Magazine* July 1893,
Uncollected Stories 1971) is a reminiscence about a
friend lost in battle. It is told by the village black-
smith to the horsewoman-narrator while he tends
her horse.

The Irish stories are effective at capturing the
flavor and atmosphere of Irish immigrant life. The
use of Irish dialect is especially well done. "The Luck
of the Bogans" (*Scribner's Magazine* January 1889,
Strangers and Wayfarers 1890) is perhaps the best of
these. Mike Bogan, his wife, Biddy Flaherty, and
their child leave their home in Bantry, Ireland, to
emigrate to the United States. As they leave, Peggy
Muldoon, the old beggar woman of Bantry, loudly
laments their departure, predicting doom. She is
accompanied by Marget Dunn, Biddy O'Hern and
"no-legged Tom Whinn, the fragment of a once
active sailor who propelled himself by a low truckle
cart and two short sticks." In America Mike opens a
liquor store and is reasonably successful, except that
his son, "the luck of the Bogans," turns into a
ne'er-do-well who drinks excessively and is eventually killed in a bar fight. The broken-hearted father
smashes all the bottles in his store and destroys the
liquor kegs.

"A Little Captive Maid" (*Scribner's Magazine*
December 1891, *A Native of Winby* 1893) also opens
in Ireland. Nora Connelly is leaving Johnny Morris,
her lover, to come to the United States to make her
fortune. Afterwards she plans to return to Ireland
and marry Johnny. In America she becomes a maid
to Captain Balfour, a retired sea captain. When he
dies, he leaves her five hundred pounds and passage
money to Ireland, as she has been homesick during
her entire stay abroad. She returns to Ireland,
where Johnny is still waiting, and they marry and
start their life together providentially, thanks to

Nora's success. The final Irish story of this period is "Between Mass and Vespers" (*Scribner's Magazine* May 1893, *A Native of Winby* 1893). It concerns the trials and tribulations of Father Ryan, the parish priest, in particular his successful attempt to make one of his parishioners repent.

5

The Country of the Pointed Firs
and Other Late Works:
1896–1910

Sarah Orne Jewett's masterpiece, *The Country of the Pointed Firs* (1896), was completed at the height of her career. It is a consummation of the thematic and formal concerns that had shaped her work since *Deephaven*. In her preface to the 1925 edition, Willa Cather ranked it as one of three American works destined for literary immortality, the other two of which were *The Scarlet Letter* and *Huckleberry Finn*.

The work is structurally innovative. More unified than a collection of sketches, yet looser than the traditional novel, it is difficult to classify by genre. Its "plot," like that of *Deephaven*, is held together by a unique structural device: the presence of two women at a series of events and the growth of their relationship with one another. Unlike *Deephaven*, however, *The Country of the Pointed Firs* does not suffer from clashes of mood between the women and their environment. On the contrary, a correspondence exists between the moral and physical landscapes in the work that at times takes on symbolic significance.

Aesthetic control is maintained throughout. There is consistency in imagery and clear thematic counterpoint. All of this contributes to the work's remarkable effect of aesthetic integrity, one important reason for its claim to the honor of "master-piece."

Themes that emerged as central in earlier works are important here as well: the tensions between rural and urban, and among independence, isolation and community. But in this work they assume greater significance. In *The Country of the Pointed Firs* they are expressed as an underlying conflict between time passing—both of history and of personal relationships—and time transcended. The narrator seems to be seeking some meaning beyond the fleetingness and fragility of human bonds. The sea-coast area of Maine is for her an example of a community that transcends individual barriers. This model of transcendence is the most important moral idea presented in the work; it brings to final synthesis Jewett's continuing theme of isolation and community.

At the same time and on another plane, Dunnet Landing, the remote hamlet the narrator visits, seems to be a town on the edge of historical time. Mrs. Todd, the town herbalist, practices rites that belong to lost ages. Other characters hearken back to timeless states; one speaks of a land that exists between the living and the dead, between time and eternity. Mrs. Todd and her ancient craft—indeed the entire "country of the pointed firs"—provide an alternative that transcends the powers of Western industrial "progress" that Jewett has seen encroaching on her pastoral sanctuary.

While in earlier works Jewett's tone was optimistic, in *The Country of the Pointed Firs* it is elegaic. The preindustrial, matriarchal community of Dunnet Landing is dying, and in what is undoubtedly her greatest work Sarah Orne Jewett grieves its passing as an historical entity, but celebrates its eternity as a way of being.

The work has had a peculiar publishing

history.[1] It was originally published in four sections, in the January, March, July and September 1896 issues of the *Atlantic Monthly*. In this original form it comprised twenty chapters. In the transition to the book edition, published the same year by Houghton Mifflin, Jewett added the two final chapters, "Along Shore" and "A Backward Glance" and compressed what had been chapters 18 and 19 into one, entitled "The Bowden Reunion." She also added the chapter titles at this time. Three years later Jewett published two more stories that were set in Dunnet Landing and that featured some of the same characters as *The Country of the Pointed Firs:* these were "The Queen's Twin" (*Atlantic Monthly* February 1899 and *Cornhill Magazine* February 1899, *The Queen's Twin* 1899) and "A Dunnet Shepherdess" (*Atlantic Monthly* December 1899, *The Queen's Twin* 1899). In 1900 "The Foreigner" (*Atlantic Monthly* August 1900, *Uncollected Stories* 1971) was published. "William's Wedding," another sketch in this group, was unfinished at Jewett's death in 1909.

In 1910 Houghton Mifflin published a seven-volume edition of Jewett's works entitled *Stories and Tales*. In this edition of *The Country of the Pointed Firs*, "A Dunnet Shepherdess" and "William's Wedding" were added between what had been the penultimate and the last chapter of the work. In 1919 "The Queen's Twin" was added as chapter 23. The Willa Cather edition of 1925 included these three stories. Since then this has been the standard edition of *The Country of the Pointed Firs*. This discussion of the work, however, follows the original organization, treating first the four sections published in the *Atlantic Monthly* in 1896 and then discussing separately the stories published subsequently.

The first published section included chapters 1 through 7. The first chapter describes the return late in June of a middle-aged woman to Dunnet

Landing, a seacoast village in Maine that she had
visited briefly a few years previously. This character, who narrates the story, is a writer and evidently a
Jewett persona. It is not entirely clear why she has
come to this remote hamlet; partly it is because she
has fallen "in love" with its charm.

When one really knows a village like this and its surroundings, it is like becoming acquainted with a single person.
The process of falling in love at first sight is as final as it is
swift in such a case, but the growth of true friendship may
be a lifelong affair.

Partly we sense that the narrator is in the midst of a
spiritual crisis and has come to this rural area seeking spiritual regeneration. This she finds.

In the second chapter, the visitor secures lodging with Mrs. Almira Todd. Since it is the beginning
of the herb-gathering season, Mrs. Todd must
spend much time in the fields; therefore, her guest
volunteers to help her by waiting on customers and
patients during the day. This keeps her from her
writing, however; so she finds she must seclude herself from "seein' folks" in order to work. The desire
to socialize conflicts with the need for solitude. In
the evenings, however, the women have time together for long conversations over the spruce beer
that Mrs. Todd brews. A sense of intimacy, deep
feeling and trust develops between the women.

The narrator has already begun to see Mrs.
Todd as a person with supernatural powers. Her
herbal art seems a kind of mysterious witchcraft.
The herbs arouse a sense of a power that transcends
time.

There were some strange and pungent odors that roused
a dim sense and remembrance of something in the forgotten past. Some of these might once have belonged to
sacred and mystic rites, and have had some occult knowledge handed with them down the centuries . . . .

Mrs. Todd ministers not only to the townspeople's physical ills, but to their social and psychological problems as well. "It seemed sometimes as if love and hate and jealousy and adverse winds at sea might also find their proper remedies among the curious wild-looking plants in Mrs. Todd's garden." Like Miss Tempy, Mrs. Todd has the power to cast spells over people, and she does so over her summer guest. In their late night talks Mrs. Todd sometimes "told . . . all that lay deepest in her heart." The narrator learns that in Almira's youth she had suffered an unrequited love from which she had never recovered, even after her marriage. In the dim light Mrs. Todd takes on the "massiveness" of "a huge sibyl," the first of several classical allusions Jewett used to accentuate the power and agelessness of her central character.

The next two chapters concern the narrator's attempt to distance herself from the hubbub of Mrs. Todd's commerce by renting a schoolhouse for the summer in which to do her writing (something Jewett herself did). One afternoon in July she looks out the schoolhouse window to watch a funeral procession in the town below, a scene reminiscent of that in "The King of Folly Island." This evokes feelings of isolation in the observer. By cutting herself off from this social event "I had now made myself and my friends remember that I did not really belong to Dunnet Landing." She notes how the procession "looked futile and helpless on the edge of the rocky shore" and in the presence of eternity.

Chapters 5 and 6 are given to a strange narrative by Captain Littlepage, a lonely old retired sea captain, who looks like "an aged grasshopper" and has a "cant to leeward" like wind-blown coastal vegetation. The captain mounted up to the schoolhouse after the funeral to chat with the town visitor. Before his arrival the narrator had been meditating on the passage of time: "an hour was very long in that coast town where nothing stole away the shortest minute." She feels herself to be "a besieged miser of time" in her quest for hours in which to write.

Captain Littlepage's tale is thus set in the context of the subject of time. The captain himself seems like a creature out of ages past. His narrative concerns a sea voyage he once took on which he claims to have discovered the secret of the afterlife. In the course of his story he takes the occasion to lament the degeneration of Dunnet Landing in recent years since the decline of the shipping trade. Now it is "full of loafers." No one any longer has firsthand knowledge of the outside world; one has to rely instead on "cheap, unprincipled newspaper":

There's no large-minded way of thinking now: the worst have got to be best and rule everything; we're all turned upside down and going back year by year.

After his diatribe against the machine age they sit silently and hear "the noise of the water on a beach below. It sounded like the strange warning wave that gives notice of the turn of the tide." At the same time, nearer at hand "a late golden robin, with the most joyful and eager of voices, was singing close by in a thicket of wild roses." These two images, the wave and the robin, seem to symbolize the two states that are at odds with one another in this work; the wave suggesting the movement of history, and the robin, the ageless pastoral world that transcends time.

Littlepage's narrative "The Waiting Place" describes his experiences after being shipwrecked on a voyage in Arctic waters. Only he and one other crewman were saved. They found refuge at a Moravian missionary settlement, where Littlepage was housed with a half-deranged Scotsman named Gaffett, who had also been lost at sea years before.

Gaffett told the newcomer of a strange voyage he had taken into far Arctic reaches and of "a strange sort of country 'way up north beyond the ice, and strange folks living in it." The strange folks were shades, "all blowing gray figures," "fog-shaped men." Gaffett and his mates came to believe it was "a kind of waiting-place between this world an' the next."

Littlepage's "waiting-place" is another image of a timeless place beyond the reaches of history. The seventh and final chapter in this first section presents another such image, that of a distant offshore island where Mrs. Todd's mother resides. As Mrs. Todd and the narrator stand looking out to sea one afternoon, a sunburst lights up a far island and makes it "seem like a sudden revelation of the world beyond this which some believe to be so near. 'That's where mother lives,' said Mrs. Todd."

That evening the women are together once again. Their intimacy presents yet another instance of transcendence, perhaps the most significant in the work—and to Jewett herself, that provided by community. The narrator draws the connection between Littlepage's timeless realm and the sanctuary created between the two women in Mrs. Todd's humble cottage. "I felt for a moment as if it were part of a spell and incantation, and as if my enchantress would now begin to look like the cobweb shapes of the arctic town."

The second published section of *The Country of the Pointed Firs* includes chapters 8 through 11, which concern a one-day visit the two women make by boat to Green Island, where Mrs. Todd's mother, Mrs. Blackett, and her son William live. This section presents images of community that contrast with the half-mad isolation of Captain Littlepage. (He is later described as one for whom "the world were a great mistake and he had nobody with whom to speak his own language or find companionship.") The Green Island section is also set as a contrast to the following section, which concerns another isolate, Joanna. Jewett established a thematic counterpoint by alternating examples of isolation in one section with models of community in the next. This broad pattern continues throughout the work, with minor variations played out within sections.

Mrs. Blackett, who is eighty-six years old, is an exemplar of the Jewett woman who single-handedly sustains a sense of community in the area. As such, she is the most important character in the work after Mrs. Todd. Although she lives in physical isolation, Mrs. Blackett is one of those "who do not live to themselves, . . . who have long since passed the line that divides mere self-concern from a valued share in whatever Society can give and take." In a later section, which describes a family reunion, we see how faces light up at the sight of Mrs. Blackett and how her spiritual presence has maintained the coastal community despite physical separation. "One revelation after another was made of the constant interest and intercourse that had linked the far island and these scattered farms into a golden chain of love and dependence."

William, her son, at the age of sixty retains an air of pastoral innocence. He is shy and speaks little, but he does give the narrator a tour around the island, showing her some of its magnificent vistas. These provide another image of timelessness: "It gave a sudden sense of space, for nothing stopped the eye or hedged one in—that sense of liberty in space and time which great prospects always give."

After a lunch of Mrs. Blackett's fish chowder, Mrs. Todd takes the narrator on a herb-gathering expedition in quest of pennyroyal. On the way she reveals more about her past. Her husband Nathan had been lost in a shipwreck not far from the island.

She suggests, however, that had he lived he might have learned her secret, that her heart still belonged to her earlier love. With these words "an absolute, archaic grief possessed this countrywoman; she seemed like a renewal of some historic soul, with her sorrows and the remoteness of a daily life busied with rustic simplicities and the scents of primeval herbs."

The day ends sentimentally as the family gathers to sing old songs. Mrs. Todd and her guest return home that evening laden with lobsters, new potatoes, and salted mackerel. Even Dunnet Landing seems noisy and bustling after the peace of Green Island.

The third published section of *The Country of the Pointed Firs* (chapters 12 through 15) is about one of Jewett's most extreme isolates, Joanna the hermit. Her story is framed, however, in the context of a community setting. Mrs. Fosdick, an old friend of Mrs. Todd's, has settled in for a visit. One evening, while a northeaster is blowing outside, the women sit around the Franklin stove and reminisce. Mrs Fosdick, like Captain Littlepage, laments how "everybody's just like everybody else, now." This triggers a recollection of Joanna Todd, whatever else one may wish to say about her, was an original.

Joanna is one of the group of Jewett characters, discussed in the last chapter, who isolate themselves from the rest of the world out of spite. In her case the spite is directed against herself. In her youth she had been "crossed in love" and in a moment of extreme disappointment had blasphemed God. As self-flagellation for this "unpardonable sin" she moved to barren Shell-heap Island and refused to see friends or family until her death twenty years later.

Mrs. Todd recollects that, because Joanna was a cousin of her husband, she and a Reverend Mr.

Dimmock had made a voyage out to the island to attempt to persuade Joanna to return. Mrs. Todd's attitude toward ministers turns out to be similar to Mrs. Goodsoe's towards doctors: they know little of true caring. The minister attempts to scare Joanna back by giving her a fire-and-brimstone lecture, which she ignores. Almira then has a long talk with her, begging her to return or to live on Green Island with Mrs. Blackett, but Joanna refuses. Mrs. Todd had brought Joanna a coral pin her husband had purchased abroad for his cousin; Joanna gives it back to Almira and asks her to keep it.

Mrs. Todd then remembers Joanna's funeral, which was held on the island, and recalls that a small sparrow who lit on Joanna's coffin did a better job of eulogizing her than did Reverend Dimmock. Later the narrator makes a pilgrimage to Joanna's shrine of solitude on Shell-heap Island. She notes that

in the life of each of us . . . there is a place remote and islanded, and given to endless regret or secret happiness; we are each the uncompanioned hermit and recluse of an hour or a day; we understand our fellows of the cell to whatever age of history they may belong.

Joanna represents a state of being.

The final section of the work, which includes chapters 16 through 19, deals with the Bowden Family Reunion. This event, which occurs in mid-August, is the high point of the narrator's stay in the area and presents the central image of community in the work. The narrator elevates the happening to a level of religious significance.

Such a day as this has transfiguring powers. [It] gives to those who are dumb their chance to speak, and lends some beauty to the plainest face.

Such communal experiences bring us out of our fallen states of being and put us in touch with a sense of the sacred. There is, moreover, a matriarchal quality about the event. Mrs. Blackett reigns supreme: " 'Mother's always the queen,' said Mrs. Todd." The old Bowden house seems like "a motherly brown hen waiting for the flock."

The reunion procession counterpoints the funeral procession seen in the first section; the present event is, however, in celebration of life. Nevertheless like all social rituals it brings its participants into touch with a timeless realm and gives them a sense of belonging to an ancient tradition.

We might have been a company of ancient Greeks going to celebrate a victory, or to worship the gods of harvests in the grove above. It was strangely moving to see this and to make part of it. The sky, the sea, have watched poor humanity at its rites so long; we were no more a New England family celebrating its own existence and simple progress; we carried the tokens and inheritance of all such households from which this had descended, and were only the latest of our line. We possessed the instincts of a far, forgotten childhood . . . .

Significantly, the narrator feels herself to be a part of the community for the first time, in contrast to her feeling of distance from the funeral. This seems to resolve the perennial Jewett dilemma between being an outsider to or a native of rural Maine.

The narrator is moved to meditate further on the effect such a communal affair has on its participants, in particular Mrs. Todd:

I could see that sometimes when Mrs. Todd had seemed limited and heavily domestic, she had simply grown sluggish for lack of proper surroundings.

. . . .

It was not the first time that I was full of wonder at the waste of human ability in this world, as a botanist wonders at the wastefulness of nature, the thousand seeds that die, the unused provision of every sort.

Once again we see that what had been perceived in earlier works as a condition of rural life to be escaped at all costs—its limited emotional and career opportunities—in *The Country of the Pointed Firs* is a condition of life, created by social circumstances perhaps, yet redeemable by the experience of community.

After the return to Dunnet Landing the narrator encounters one more memorable character, Elijah Tilley, before her departure. Tilley is a fisherman who is still mourning his wife eight years after her death. He lives in lonely isolation.

It is late summer and the time has come for the writer–narrator to return to her home, which is presumably in a city, Boston or New York. She has so assimilated herself to the peace and simplicity of life in Dunnet Landing that she fears being a "foreigner" back in her own world. On the day of her departure by steamer Mrs. Todd is irritable, obviously hiding her grief at the loss of her friend. The parting scene between them is filled with unspoken emotion.

With this last word Mrs. Todd turned and left me as if with sudden thought of something she had forgotten, so that I felt sure she was coming back, but presently I heard her go out of the kitchen door and walk down the path toward the gate. I could not part so; I ran after her to say good-by, but she shook her head and waved her hand without looking back when she heard my hurrying steps, and so went away down the street.

The visitor realizes that this episode in her life has ended. "So we die before our own eyes; so we see some chapters of our lives come to their natural end." Almira had left her a few gifts on the kitchen table. Among them is Joanna's coral pin. As the narrator leaves, she catches sight of Mrs. Todd:

"Her distant figure looked mateless and appealing, with something about it that was strangely self-possessed and mysterious." Thus the final image of the book is one of separation, solitude and mortality. Yet the world that the narrator has been part of for that summer is one of a community that transcends the passage of human time and the frailty of human bonds.

In addition to the work's thematic coherence, artistic unity is created by its remarkable imagery —especially its metaphors. Aristotle claimed that a command of metaphor is the mark of genius. If this be the requisite, Sarah Orne Jewett certainly belongs in the ranks. In *The Country of the Pointed Firs* the imagery falls into two classes: one that uses materials from the seacoast environment and one that depends upon classical literary allusions. An example of the former is the following:

when . . . a certain Mrs. Fosdick appeared like a strange sail on the far horizon, I suffered much from apprehension. I had been living in the quaint little house with as much comfort and unconsciousness as if it were a larger body, or a double shell, in whose simple convolutions Mrs. Todd and I had secreted ourselves, until some wandering hermit crab of a visitor marked the little spare room for her own.

The appropriateness of the metaphor both to the environment and to the feelings the narrator wishes to express are the mark of an artist who is in firm command of her craft and who has an intimate and authentic knowledge of her materials.

Examples of the other trope employed in the work include the following descriptions of the central character:

Mrs. Todd had mounted a gray rock, and stood there grand and architectural, like a *caryatide*.

There was something lonely and solitary about her great
determined shape. She might have been Antigone alone
on the Theban plain.

Such figures elevate the character to the level of the
universal and legendary.

As with many of Jewett's other works, there has
been considerable speculation as to where *The Country of the Pointed Firs* is geographically set. In the
case of this work such theorizing seems particularly
inappropriate, because it exists as a self-contained
fictional universe within which the physical realities
take on symbolic significance. (This is of course true
of all works of fiction, but some are more self-
referential than others). Nevertheless, it is believed
that the land of the "pointed firs" is located on
Maine's St. George Peninsula and that Martinsville
was the model for Dunnet Landing. Jewett and
Annie Fields had vacationed there shortly before
the book was written. Jewett herself took her usual
stance: Dunnet Landing was not a real place. "I
cannot tell you where Dunnets [*sic*] Landing is except that it must be somewhere 'along shore' between the region of Tenant's Harbor and Boothbay
. . . ." She once told Henry James that in fact the
work had been "chiefly written" before she had ever
visited the Martinsville area.[2]

From the beginning, the book received a fa-
vorable critical reception. The initial reviews were
unanimous in their praise for Jewett's "true and
delicate art."[3] Over the years important critics have
agreed that *The Country of the Pointed Firs* is a
significant work of American literature, probably
the masterpiece of the local color school.[4]

Two additional stories set in Dunnet Landing
and featuring Mrs. Todd appeared in 1899 in the
Atlantic Monthly. These were "A Dunnet Shepher-

dess" and "The Queen's Twin." In the former story William and the narrator go trout fishing "up-country" where they spend the afternoon with Mrs. Hight, a crippled widow, and her daughter Esther. Esther is a shepherdess. She is a personification of pastoral innocence and looks from a distance "like a figure of Millet's." There appears to be a blossoming romance between Esther and William. This story is somewhat marred by a profusion of classical and literary allusions, a tendency held barely in check in *The Country of the Pointed Firs*.

The love affair between Esther and William is developed as the central event of "William's Wedding," a sketch never finished but published in 1910. In this piece the narrator returns to Dunnet Landing the following May. Her reunion with Mrs. Todd is described in highly emotional terms: her heart "was beating like a lover's" as she approached the woman's cottage. She had returned to coastal Maine to get away from the city's irrelevant distractions; once back in Dunnet Landing she feels "solid and definite again, instead of a poor, incoherent being."

The wedding between Esther and William is briefly described: it is a scene of radiant innocence, symbolized by the lamb the bride carries throughout the nuptial day. Mrs. Todd and the narrator hold hands as they watch Esther and William depart for Green Island. The relationship between the two women tends to overshadow the wedding in this story; one senses that Jewett's real interest was in the women.

"The Queen's Twin" also concentrates on Mrs. Todd. The narrator reminds us once again of her "great soul." But the central figure in the story is Abby Martin, an elderly woman who lives inland and features herself as Queen Victoria's twin. Both were

born on the same day; both married a man named
Albert. Mrs. Martin's parlor is covered with pictures
of the queen. Mrs. Todd acknowledges, "I don't
know but Mis' Martin might be called a little peculiar." But, as she has had a hard life, Almira recognizes that her fantasy has helped her through her
troubles. "I expect all this business about the Queen
has buoyed her over many a shoal place in life."

Warner Berthoff has correctly assessed "The
Foreigner," the other Almira Todd story, as "one of
the mislaid treasures of American writing."[5] This
story, originally published in 1900, was "lost," that
is, never reprinted, until 1962 when David Bonnell
Green included it in his collection *The World of Dunnet Landing*.[6] It was also included in Richard Cary's
1971 *The Uncollected Stories of Sarah Orne Jewett*. It is
odd that this story, by far the best of the additional
Pointed Firs stories, was not included in the ex-
panded edition.

The narrative structure is similar to the second
section of the original work, that in which Joanna's
story is told. A "nor'easter" is raging outside; Mrs.
Todd and the narrator are sitting close by the fire. It
is late summer. Almira remembers that Eliza Tolland died on such a night as this some forty years
previously.

Eliza had been a young widow, reduced to danc-
ing to earn money, when some Dunnet sea captains
chanced upon her in Jamaica. One of them, Captain
John Tolland, decides to rescue her by marrying
her. Thus she is brought to Dunnet Landing. She
speaks little English and seems strange to the inhabitants of the town. One day she even dances in
the church, which provokes a minor scandal. But
Mrs. Blackett, ever the compassionate harmonizer,
insists that Almira look after this "stranger in a
strange land." This Almira does reluctantly, but her

hospitality reaps considerable benefits. She learns much about herbs from Eliza, who also works "charms" in her home. After Captain Tolland is lost at sea, Eliza becomes more and more isolated.

Almira is with her the night of her death. Suddenly, as she is dying, Eliza sits bolt upright and stretches her arms to the door. Mrs. Todd looks: there is "a woman's dark face lookin' right at us . . . a pleasant enough face, shaped somethin' like Mis' Tolland's." Eliza recognizes it as her dead mother. " ' "You saw her, didn't you?" she said . . . an' I says, *"Yes, dear, I did; you ain't never goin' to feel strange an' lonesome no more."* An' then in a few quiet minutes 't was all over. I felt they'd gone away together.' " Mrs. Todd adds, " 'you know plain enough there's somethin' beyond this world.' " Mrs. Todd later learns that she is the beneficiary of Mrs. Tolland's will.

In this story the matriarchal character of Jewett's world is most pronounced. Transcendence and redemption are associated with the salvific maternal figure of Mrs. Tolland's mother. Not only does Mrs. Todd and Mrs. Blackett's charitable behavior save Eliza from total isolation in life, in death she is welcomed to the world beyond by another female figure. We also see another instance of the matrilineal connection in that one woman, Mrs. Tolland, bequests her wealth and knowledge to a younger woman, Mrs. Todd. Here as throughout Jewett's work it is women who are most in touch with the supernatural and who provide transcendence.

It is possible that the germ of this story came from the example of Jewett's close friend poet Celia Thaxter (1835–1894). According to her granddaughter and biographer, Rosamond Thaxter, Celia's "devotion to her mother had in many ways taken the place of any set religious faith."[7] She was heartbroken at her mother's death and held seances to try to reach her. At Celia's death her brother announced, "Mother came in the night and took sister away" (p. 349). (It is also possible that "The King of Folly Island" was based in some measure on the Thaxter family; Celia's father had been known as "The King of the Island Empire,"[8] a reference to his economic rule over the Isles of Shoals, an archipelago off the coasts of Maine and New Hampshire.)

During Jewett's final years of literary output she produced at least three outstanding stories and several others of some interest, as well as her historical novel, *The Tory Lover.* She had published numerous verses during her literary career, none of exceptional artistic interest, although "The Gloucester Mother," (*McClure's Magazine* October 1908) had a certain popularity. A selection of her poems was published posthumously as *Verses* in 1916. Several of her unpublished poems, most of which are in the Houghton Library, are, however, of considerable biographical interest. They are love poems written to women, in particular to Annie Fields.[9]

The three exceptional stories written in Jewett's final years are: "The Green Bowl" (*New York Herald* 3 November 1901, *Uncollected Stories* 1971), "Aunt Cynthy Dallett," originally published as "The New-Year Guests" (*Harper's Bazar* 11 January 1896, *The Queen's Twin* 1899), and "Martha's Lady," (*Atlantic Monthly* October 1897, *The Queen's Twin* 1899). They continue the themes of matrilineality and female friendship.

"The Green Bowl" is one of Jewett's most eccentric tales of the supernatural. It is narrated by two young women, Frances Kent and Kate Montagne, to several older people in a manner reminiscent of *Deephaven.* The two women had a habit of taking horse and buggy trips through the country, somewhat adventurously staying at whatever inns they happened upon. One evening a heavy rainstorm breaks and they seek shelter in a rural church, putting their horse in a nearby shed. They are able to build a fire in the church stove; they have food with them and they lock the church doors against "burglars" and so are secure for the night.

The next morning the church caretaker, Mrs. Patton, invites them to her farm for breakfast. While there, they notice two green bowls on a shelf. Mrs. Patton tells them that the bowls are charmed. A wild seaman had brought them back from China to her great-aunt, who kept them for fifty years during which time she and the seaman were "companions": they held the prophetic powers that came from owning the bowls.

Next Mrs. Patton and one other person became companions and held the fortune-telling gift: however, Mrs. Patton's companion died two days before her meeting with Kate and therefore must be replaced. The old woman determines that the fates have sent her Kate to be her companion, and she gives Kate the green bowl. Mrs. Patton had demonstrated her powers by telling the girls information about themselves that she could have received only by psychic means.

After Kate relates this story, she gazes at the bowl and suddenly realizes that she too has the gift. A vision of her listeners appears, and she sees that one of them is about to die. She is shocked but says nothing. Her urbane "enlightened" audience debunks the story. Once again we find Jewett associating psychic powers with rural women who are far from the influence of "civilized" rationalism. The matrilineal connection is seen in the passage of the "gift" from Mrs. Patton to Kate.

"Aunt Cynthy Dallett" concerns two women who agree to live together. The protagonist is an eighty-five-year-old woman who had lived alone up

a mountain for many years. Her niece, Abby Pen-
dexter, has kept track of her but is finding it increas-
ingly difficult in winter months to carry out her
responsibility. Abby is poor and has recently had to
sell her hens just to pay the rent. Both prefer living
alone but recognize the mutual advantages of living
together. Abby agrees to move up to Aunt Cynthy's
and Aunt Cynthy in turn announces that she is leaving her home and possessions to Abby.

"Martha's Lady," perhaps Jewett's single
greatest story, is reminiscent of Flaubert's "Un
Coeur Simple," which describes the intense religious devotion of a simple peasant woman to a par-
rot in terms that suggest the emotional dynamics of
any religious obsession. Jewett's story is less ironic,
as the object of the devotion is another person, and
more elegaic, for the waste of human emotional
potential.

Martha is a servant in the house of Miss Harriet
Pyne. She is "tall, ungainly" and "clumsy." Harriet's
young cousin Helena Vernon comes to visit one
summer. She is full of enthusiasm and helps Martha
to learn some of her tasks. Because of Helena's faith
in her, Martha "knew what love was like." Martha
weeps when Helena departs and vows to think of her
every day.

Her devotion to Helena grows over the years,
taking on religious fervor. Her thoughts of Helena
became "like a saint's vision." Meanwhile Helena
marries and travels the world. Martha cries when
she learns of Helena's marriage. She "felt a strange
sense of loss and pain. . . . Her idol seemed to be less
her own since she had become the idol of a
stranger." Nevertheless, her faith remains strong,
and, when, forty years later, Helena returns, she
understands Martha's devotion. "She suddenly
knew the whole story and could hardly speak." Of

this story Jewett once revealingly commented, "nobody must say that Martha was dull, it is only I."

Of the other stories written during this period, some continue the themes of courtship and marriage, such as "A Change of Heart" (*Ladies' Home Journal* April 1896, *Uncollected Stories* 1971) and "A Pinch of Salt" (*Boston Evening Transcript* 30 October 1897, *Uncollected Stories* 1971). The last story Jewett published in her lifetime, "A Spring Sunday" (*McClure's Magazine* May 1904, *Uncollected Stories* 1971) is a nostalgic celebration of a successful marriage.

A lengthy feud is ended in " The Lost Turkey" (*Youth's Companion* 27 November 1902, *Uncollected Stories,* 1971). A woman is brought out of self-inflicted isolation in "Sister Peacham's Turn" (*Harper's Magazine* November 1902, *Uncollected Stories* 1971). And a family recognizes its rural identity, giving up wealth and society to return to country living in "A Born Farmer" (*McClure's Magazine* June 1901, *Uncollected Stories* 1971).

There are several more Irish stories, bringing to seven the total of stories about Irish immigrants that Jewett wrote. One of these, "The Gray Mills of Farley" (*The Cosmopolitan* June 1898, *Uncollected Stories* 1971), was one of Jewett's few stories to describe realistically the inhuman conditions of a New England manufacturing town. The "gray houses" "had no room for gardens or even for little green sideyards where one might spend a summer evening." The inhabitants are at the mercy of the capitalist-owners. Jewett's position in this story is decidely prolabor and anticapitalist. The other Irish stories are "Where's Nora?" (*Scribner's Magazine* December 1898, *Uncollected Stories* 1971); "Bold Words at the Bridge" (*McClure's Magazine* April 1899, *Uncollected Stories* 1971), and "Elleneen" (*McClure's Magazine*

February 1901, *Uncollected Stories* 1971).

Had Sarah Orne Jewett known that she had but few years left to write, she perhaps would have spent her time on something other than *The Tory Lover*. It is clearly a diversion from the mainstream of her work, written by someone who anticipates returning to her real work later. But it remains her last full-length work, published in 1901. Critics have not been kind to the novel, perhaps because they take it too seriously. But it has proved to be the most popular of Jewett's works. It went into five printings in its first three months. A bicentennial edition was published in 1976. It is still promoted in bookstores in the Piscataqua region where Jewett is known primarily for its authorship.

The novel is a historical romance based on local New England history. It could easily be transposed into a Class B motion picture. Set during the Revolutionary War, it includes romantic scenes at sea, trysts, and dances, as well as mob scenes and a scene in prison. The plot concerns the romance between Mary Hamilton, a handsome young aristocrat, who is a Patriot, that is, loyal to the colonies, and Roger Wallingford, also of the upper classes, who wavers between loyalty to the crown (or Toryism) and loyalty to the new confederation. Under Mary's influence Roger becomes a Patriot and signs an oath to this effect. His mother, however, who is probably the most interesting figure in the novel, remains loyal to King George, refuses to sign the oath, and for this has her house attacked and barely escapes to England alive. Jewett's sympathies seem to lie on the Tory side (some of her own ancestors had been Tories); her depiction of Madame Wallingford is most sympathetic.

To prove his patriotism Roger signs up with John Paul Jones's ship the *Ranger,* which sails for

France from Portsmouth, New Hampshire, in the fall of 1777, presumably to attempt to persuade France to ally with the colonies against England. In April 1778 the *Ranger* moves on to England where it carries out some minor marauding on the coast. While there, one of Wallingford's enemies, Dickson, leaves him on shore wounded. Dickson returns to the ship and announces that Wallingford has defected. Wallingford is meanwhile thrown into an English prison.

Back in Portsmouth and Berwick the news of Roger's alleged treason is received. Madame Wallingford's home is attacked and she and Mary leave for England on the *Golden Dolphin* in search of Roger. Eventually all ends happily. Roger is exonerated. His enemy is discovered. He and Mary return together to the colonies.

Jewett herself acknowledged that the novel did not live up to her expectations. "I grow very melancholy if I fall to thinking of the distance between my poor story and the first dreams of it." Henry James's comment was perhaps the most to the point: "Go back," he pleaded, "to the dear Country of the Pointed Firs, *come* back to the palpable present *intimate* that throbs responsive, and that wants, misses, needs you, God knows, and suffers woefully in your absence."[10] But Sarah Orne Jewett was never to return to the land where her greatest work had been set. After her fall from a carriage in 1902, which severely incapacitated her, she never again completed a work of fiction. In June 1909 she died of a cerebral hemorrhage.

6

Criticism and Influence

Sarah Orne Jewett never wrote a sustained piece of critical theory. Yet her letters contain nuggets of critical comment from which may be construed the fundamentals of her own theory of art. These come mainly in the form of advice to younger writers, such as Willa Cather (1876–1947), who in the early twentieth century was just beginning her literary career. We also have a series of critical remarks Jewett made in letters about literary works, often classics, that she was reading. These too give us a clear idea of what she valued in literature and help to explain what she attempted in her own fiction. Her ideas are sometimes classical, sometimes Romantic; sometimes they even approach the poetical doctrine of the Symbolists.

Probably the most revealing comments are those she made in the series of eleven letters she wrote between 1899 and 1901 to John Thaxter (1854-1929), an unpublished novelist and short-story writer, and the son of poet Celia Thaxter.[1] He had sent Jewett several manuscripts to criticize, and she did so quite candidly. Her comments in these letters suggest a fundamentally classical taste. Her critical precepts come close to being Aristotelian: the chief values are simplicity, unity, integrity and the veracity of mimesis, or "realism."

123

Thaxter's first story she criticizes for its failure of "construction." There are "too many" characters "for the length of the story and, if I may speak plainly, too many *starts* which do not come to sufficient importance ... you keep making new claims upon the reader's attention . . . ." She urges Thaxter "to simplify it." As the story stands it is "confused and bewildering and even improbable . . . ." She adds, "I wish that you would try something that does not aim so much at incidents. Take a simpler history of life . . . ." Jewett's preference clearly is for the unified effect of classical literature. As in Aristotle's *Poetics,* the sourcebook of classical critical ideas, unity of plot and of effect are central precepts.

Earlier, Jewett had criticized Harriet Beecher Stowe's sentimental novel *The Pearl of Orr's Island* for its lack of integrity.

Alas, that she couldn't finish it in the same noble key of simplicity and harmony; but a poor writer is at the mercy of much unconscious opposition. You must throw everything and everybody aside at times, but a woman made like Mrs. Stowe cannot bring herself to that cold selfishness of the moment for one's work's sake, and the recompense for her loss is a divine touch here and there in an incomplete piece of work.[2]

Here Jewett rightly observes that a great work of literature must have a consistency in design, a unity of thought from beginning to end. Stowe's novel suffered from a large number of improbable incidents and it lacked a clear sustaining vision or *telos.*

These remarks are also of interest as they demonstrate Jewett's awareness of a central problem the woman writer has had to face, given the other responsibilities of her role: how to shed herself of the intrusions and distractions that keep her from having the time to sustain imaginative vision. In *A Room of One's Own* (1929) Virginia Woolf identified as a crippling defect in many women writers their failure to prevent the irrelevant distractions of everyday life from interfering with the perfection of their work. Jewett is keenly aware of the problem and urges upon the young writer "a cold selfishness . . . for one's work's sake," a personal discipline that will allow for imaginative integrity.

Jewett once cautioned Laura Richards, another young writer who sought advice: "Don't scatter your fire!"[3] This blunt counsel emphasizes the importance of disciplining one's imagination. Jewett urged similarly valuable wisdom upon the young Willa Cather in 1908: she told her to get away from the exciting but distracting world of newspaper work so as to be able to "guard and mature your force, and above all, have time and quiet to perfect your work." Otherwise she warns Cather that she will make no progress as a writer, for her work is "being hindered" by the distractions of the newspaper office. "You must find a quiet place near the best companions . . . your vivid, exciting companionship in the office must not be your audience, you must find your own quiet centre of life, and write from that . . . to the human heart, the great consciousness that all humanity goes to make up."[4] When Cather finally followed this advice, her great novels began to appear.

We noted above Jewett's distaste for the "improbability" of Thaxter's story. This is another important criticism that recalls an Aristotelian precept. In a famous statement in the *Poetics* Aristotle asserted that literature should deal with the probable and the necessary, not the improbable or the unlikely; this established the classical doctrine of decorum, or appropriateness. The artist "should pre-

fer probable impossibilities to improbable possibilities," he wrote. By this he meant that highly
unlikely occurrences are not a rewarding subject for
serious literary treatment. Sarah Orne Jewett agreed. In a later letter to John Thaxter she criticized
another of his stories, again for its improbability.
"The shipwreck, the drowning; it isn't simple
enough, there is *too much* in it." It lacks verisimilitude; it is not realistic enough. While a series of
unlikely events can happen in life, literature, at least
in the classical view, deals with the probability, the
necessity of their happening. When the sense of
probability or consistency is lost, the story does not
work.

Jewett's dislike of incongruity or the grotesque
in literature is another manifestation of her classical
taste. She criticized one of Thaxter's stories for an
episode that struck her as incongruous with the tone
of the piece: a scene in which the smile of a dying
woman is transformed into a ghastly grimace by a
new set of false teeth.[5] This grotesque detail of-
fended Jewett's sensitivity: "You have written all the
rest in such a different key, and keep your reader in
a different atmosphere, and so I think the very truth
of it strikes a wrong note of 'realism'." She criticizes
another Thaxter story for having a character that is
"*too* unpleasant . . . too horrible," because such a
character jars with the rest of the piece. Again the
preference is for markedly classical restraint and for
consistency in tone and mood.

In her preface to *The Country of the Pointed Firs,*
Willa Cather noted the classical character of Jewett's
own work, a point echoed by F. O. Matthiessen in his
monumental study, *American Renaissance.*[6] Cather
cites Gilbert Murray's distinction between two kinds
of beauty; the one that comes from "rich ornamentation" as on "a Chinese junk, gorgeously gilded and

painted, hung with rich embroideries and tapestries."

Then there is the beauty of a modern yacht, where there is no ornamentation at all; . . . it has an organic, living simplicity and directness. This, he says, is the beauty for which the Greek writers strove; it is certainly that for which Miss Jewett strove.

The letters to John Thaxter and others reveal a further concern that is fundamentaal to Jewett's literary judgment: a dislike of artificiality and literary pretentiousness, which at its worst is dishonesty. She criticizes the "artificial quality in [the] makeup" of one of Thaxter's stories, and, regarding another, urges him not to "write a *'story'* but just *tell the thing!*" The latter comment, which she derived from her father, she repeated on numerous occasions. In this form Jewett clearly means that Thaxter should not attempt to create an artificial construct, "a short story," but should describe things exactly as he sees them, letting the form follow the content. In other words, she felt that structure should be organic.

One critic has remarked upon the fundamental honesty or ingenuousness of Jewett's character as it emerges in her early letters.[7] This moral trait Jewett carried over into her critical judgments and into her own literary practice. In impassioned advice to Willa Cather she urged her to live and to think on a level of the highest integrity, because this is the only way to sustain such quality in one's work.

Otherwise what might be strength in a writer is only crudeness, and what might be insight is only observation; sentiment falls to sentimentality—you can write about life, but never write life itself. And to write and work on this level, we must live on it—we must at least recognize it and defer to it at every step . . . we must be our best selves.

Another more specific criticism that Jewett made of young Cather's work at this time also raised the question of artistic honesty. In one of Cather's early stories, "On the Gulls' Road," published in *McClure's Magazine* in December 1908, Jewett detected a note of falsity. Cather's use of a male persona struck Jewett as an unnecessary bit of "masquerading"; it interfered with the integrity of the piece. Jewett commented,

the lover is as well done as he could be when a woman writes in the man's character,—it must always, I believe, be something of a masquerade. I think it is safer to write about him as you did about the others, and not try to be he! And you could almost have done it as yourself—a woman could love her in that same protecting way—a woman could even care enough to wish to take her away from such a life, by some means or other.

Again we may note Jewett's concern about maintaining a fundamental honesty in one's work, avoiding such artificial "masquerading" as bows to social convention.

It is interesting in this regard to compare Cather's masterpiece, *My Ántonia* (1918), with *The Country of the Pointed Firs*, its literary antecedent. Both present a strong female protagonist through the eyes of a nostalgic narrator who once loved her. In Jewett's case the narrator is a woman; in Cather's, a man. In Jewett's work the relationship between Almira Todd and the narrator is far more credible than the awkward connection between Jim Burden, who remains an inauthentic character, and Ántonia. Although Cather's novel is a masterwork, it is weakened by the improbability of that relationship.

Because of her insistence upon a fidelity to and an honesty with one's materials, Jewett is often classified a "realist." This label cannot be applied, however, without explanation and qualification. Realism is the term applied to a literary movement that developed in the latter half of the nineteenth century in reaction against or as an outgrowth of Romanticism. Romanticism had been the first literary reaction against industrial capitalism, and Realism carried forward its critique. Both movements decried the effects of mechanization: its reduction of products to qualitative sameness and of people to the level of products. Romantic literature tended to vaunt the value of the personal, subjective, emotional reaction and the virtues of places and times remote from the nineteenth century industrial city.

Writers in the tradition of Realism took a different tack; they chose to focus on the ugly details of contemporary life so as to evoke a similar critique in the reader's mind. And generally they preferred that the writer present material neutrally or from an "objective" point of view. Critic Warner Berthoff defined Realism as "a fundamentally moral cause, a purification of spirit; the acquisitive, merchandising society of modern times is defined as the enemy; the ancient discipline of self-governing craftsmanship is brought forward in opposition . . . ."[8] Alfred Kazin noted that the new literary movement was "alien to a domineering capitalism and half-nostalgic for a preindustrial society."[9]

Given this broad definition of Realism it is easy to place Sarah Orne Jewett within its embrace. Her father's advice, which she repeated over and over ("tell the thing as it is"), is a straightforward statement of Realist doctrine. Her attempts to control moralizing and sentimentalizing in her own stories is also a Realist impulse. Her advice to young writers to avoid artificial "literariness" and to write from experience also are hallmarks of the Realist conception of literature.

An interesting critique she once made of Nathaniel Hawthorne's *American Notebooks* (1868) shows her impatience with the sweeping sentimentalities of the Romantic vision. She decried the author's "conscious effort after material." The sketches "lack any reality or imagination, rootless little things that could never open seed in their turn . . . so 'delicate' in their fancy as to be far-fetched and oddly feeble and sophomorish." She far prefers Charles W. Brewster's *Rambles About Portsmouth* (First Series, 1859; Second Series, 1869), a completely unliterary collection of sketches; she finds it "a mine of wealth."

One description of the marketwomen coming down the river,—their quaintness and picturesqueness at once seems to be so great, and the mere hints of description so full of flavor, that it all gave me much keener pleasure than anything I found in the other much more famous book [Hawthorne's *Notebooks*].

She acknowledges that this is "high literary treason" but predicts that Brewster's work will outlive Hawthorne's because of the veracity, the lifelikeness of its detail. "Such genuine books always live, they get filled so full of life."[10]

Nevertheless, Jewett had some reservations about Realism, especially in its extreme form, Naturalism. The Naturalists, in particular Émile Zola (1840–1902) of the French school, had carried the notion of objectivity much farther than the Realists. Zola argued in *Le Roman expérimental* (1880) that the writer is analogous to the scientist: he or she should retain scientific objectivity toward the subject matter of the novel, which should be presented as scientific data derived from an experiment.

In a letter written in 1890 to Thomas Bailey Aldrich,[11] Jewett rejected the idea of "slice-of-life" objectivity and stressed that material must be presented from a particular point of view. "The trouble with most realism," she noted, "is that it isn't seen from any point of view at all, and so its shadows fall in every direction and it fails of being art." Elsewhere she commented with enthusiasm about Thackeray's *Vanity Fair,* noting how it is "full of splendid scorn for meanness and wickedness, which scorn the Zola school seems to lack." She thus implies that a moral perspective is a legitimate component of art. We have seen this principle enacted in her fiction.

In her advice to Willa Cather, Jewett stressed the importance of developing a perspective on one's material and urged Cather to distance herself from the worlds she planned to write about:

You don't see them yet quite enough from the outside, —you stand right in the middle ... without having the standpoint of the looker-on who takes them each in their relations to letters, to the world.

In other, much-cited counsel, she told Cather that she must first see the "world" before she could describe the "parish."[12]

All writers must develop distance from, or a perspective on, material that they often know intimately. As we have seen, the tension between "insider" and "outsider" knowledge was particularly acute in Sarah Orne Jewett's works. Many critics have suggested that a central difference between *Deephaven* and *The Country of the Pointed Firs* is simply that the author had had a chance to see the outer world and to mature in the time between writing the two works. In one of the earliest critical surveys of Jewett's work (1904) Charles Miner Thompson focused on the problem of point of view. He concluded (too simplistically) that Jewett had always

written as a "summer visitor" for "summer people."
Jewett read Thompson's critique, and while she rejected his terminology she acknowledged that the
question of relative proximity to or distance from
her material had always been a central issue. To
Thompson she wrote:

It was hard for this person (made of Berwick dust) to think
of herself as a "summer visitor," but I quite understand
your point . . . one may be away from one's neighborhood
long enough to see it quite or almost from the outside,
though as I make this concession I remember that it was
hardly true at the time of "Deephaven."

Jewett always insisted that the writer's point of
view is one that develops over a period of time and is
eminently personal. She once remarked to Willa
Cather: "The thing that teases the mind over and
over for years, and at last gets itself put down rightly
on paper—whether little or great, it belongs to
Literature."[13] In advice to Rose Lamb she stressed
that "one must have one's own method: it is the
personal contribution that makes true value in any
form of art or work of any sort." She had a strikingly
modern notion of the importance of the development of a unique personal style. Once she wrote of
Anne Thackeray's work: "It is, after all, Miss Thackeray herself in *Old Kensington* who gives the book its
charm."[14]

Jewett also took issue with the Realists over the
question of how much emotion was proper to literary presentation. She was not a sentimentalist, yet
she insisted on the importance of sentiment. To T.
B. Aldrich she mused, "the distinction between sentiment and sentimentality is a question of character
. . . ." And later she warned Cather against allowing
sentiment to "fall" to sentimentality. Yet she
quarrelled with William Dean Howells, who cham-

pioned himself as a Realist, over whether her own "A White Heron" was too sentimental. Howells had rejected it for publication in the *Atlantic Monthly* on those grounds. But Jewett argued: "Mr. Howells thinks that this age frowns upon the romantic, that it is no use to write romance any more; but dear me, how much of it there is left in every-day life after all." Her justification for the inclusion of sentiment, or romance, in literary works is that it is in fact realistic.

Jewett was accused by Charles Miner Thompson of taking an aristocratic position toward her material. More accurate, however, is this statement in the *Literary History of the United States:*

Of . . . Jewett one might repeat what someone said of George Sand: although she had the deepest veneration for the aristocracy of the intellect, the democracy of suffering touched her more.[15]

Several of Jewett's critical comments suggest a fundamentally democratic theory of art, one that is in the tradition of Wordsworth's preface to the second edition of the *Lyrical Ballads* (1800), an important Romantic manifesto. In this document Wordsworth had expressed the revolutionary current in Romanticism, reflecting the democratic impulse of the American and French revolutions and rejecting neoclassicism in literature, especially its penchant for upper class milieus and baroque rhetoric.

In 1885 Jewett proclaimed herself in favor of a democratic literature, a literature of the "middle ground" belonging to ordinary people.

I often think that the literary work which takes the least prominent place nowadays is that belonging to the middle ground. Scholars and so-called intellectual persons have a wealth of literature in the splendid accumulation of books that belong to all times, and now and then a new volume is added to the great list. Then there is the lowest level of literature, the trashy newspapers and sensational novels, but how seldom a book comes that stirs the minds and hearts of the good men and women of such a village as this.

She argued that if "the people" do not read good literature, it is because "few books are written for and from their standpoint." She urged that writers deal with the truth of life in "its *everyday* aspects."[16]

This she had tried to do in her own fiction. She once commented that "a dull little country village is just the place to find the real drama of life,"[17] another remark that recalls Wordsworth's injunction to the poet to choose subjects taken from "common life." Finally, she aimed at making herself accessible to "everyday" people. Her style is the language of the average reader. This, too, is in the Wordsworthian tradition of avoiding "poetic" diction and artificially literary language. (Jewett had read much Wordsworth, although once she wryly commented, "How much that we call Wordsworth himself was Dorothy to begin with." Dorothy was Wordsworth's sister.)

One final aspect of Jewett's critical theory needs to be discussed, and that is her concept of "imaginative realism," a term she used in a letter to Andress S. Floyd, another budding artist who sought her counsel.[18] By this term she meant that the writer should suggest a dimension beyond the real. In some cases this may be a moral level, as suggested by her comments on Tolstoy (see above, Chapter 2). In others it may be a level of the supernatural, as in some of her own stories. Or it may be an imaginative level, a level of emotional resonance beyond the bare facts of the story or novel. There is, she felt, a mysterious "chemistry" that makes a great work. In her

idea of "imaginative realism" Jewett approached the
poetic doctrine of the French Symbolists.

We noted in Chapter 1 Theodore Jewett's remark that the greatest compliment to a writer occurs
when the reader becomes imaginatively engaged in
the work. "A story should . . . *suggest* interesting
things to the *reader* instead of the author's doing all
the thinking for him . . . ." Once young Jewett complained that in Jane Austen's works "all the reason-
ing is done for you and all the thinking . . . . It seems
to me like hearing somebody talk on and on and on
while you have no part in the conversation, and
merely listen."[19] Jewett rejects such a passive role
for the reader.

The most appreciative reader must intuit much
of what is happening beyond the literal. Jewett com-
pliments Sarah Wyman Whitman on her sympathetic reading of "Martha's Lady": "You bring something to the reading of a story that the story would
go very lame without . . . ." She notes, "it is those
unwritable things that the story holds in its heart, if
it has any, that make the true soul of it, and these
must be understood, and yet how many a story goes
lame for lack of that understanding." She notes that
in France there is "a code" that facilitates "such
recognitions, such . . . allusions," but the American
reading public does not have such a "scaffolding"
upon which to attach interpretation. Perhaps ultimately "imaginative realism" is the quality implied
in the famous symbolist statement by Flaubert that
Jewett kept on her desk to remind her that the
writer's job is to "faire rêver": to make one dream.

Sarah Orne Jewett had a significant influence
on several important twentieth-century writers,
most of them women. Probably the most direct
influence she had was as a role model and mentor
for Willa Cather. Cather had known of Jewett in her

childhood; she remembered her face from the "Authors" card game she had played in her youth. It was not until 1908, however, that the two met.

In an interview published in 1913 Cather specified what Jewett's influence had been and why she so admired Jewett's work.[20] It was, Cather said, "that kind of honesty, that earnest endeavor to tell truly the thing that haunts the mind, that I love in Miss Jewett's own work." Cather was dismayed when she learned of Jewett's death, because she had been working on a manuscript she wished to read to her. This novel, *O Pioneers!*, was Cather's first fully successful work; it dealt with the Nebraska world that Jewett had told her to write about. Cather dedicated the work to her mentor.

I dedicated my novel *O Pioneers!* to Miss Jewett because I had talked over some of the characters in it with her . . . and in this book I tried to tell the story of the people as truthfully and simply as if I were telling it to her by word of mouth.

Jewett had taken on the function of the "ideal reader" for Cather; Cather trusted Jewett's literary sense of authenticity and quality.

Cather noted further that she had despaired of ever writing about Nebraska before she met Jewett, because she had never been able to get the stories right. "It is always hard to write about the things that are near to your heart, from a kind of instinct of self-preservation you distort them and disguise them." But Jewett read her early stories and frankly told the young writer where her work "fell short." Jewett told her that she must create her own authentic style and vision.

She said, "Write it as it is, don't try to make it like this or that. You can't do it in anybody else's way—you will have to make a way of your own. If the way happens to be new, don't let that frighten you."

Do not bow to social convention or to current literary fads, Jewett further counseled. "Don't try to write the kind of short story that this or that magazine wants—write the truth, and let them take it or leave it."

Further evidence of Jewett's influence may be seen in Cather's critical essay, "The Novel Démeublé" (1922) in which she rejects extreme forms of realism in the novel, arguing instead for a stripped-down model in which the outlines are sketched in but the details and shadings left to the imagination.

It is the inexplicable presence of the thing not named, of the overtone divined by the ear but not heard by it, the verbal mood, the emotional aura of the fact or the thing or the deed, that gives high quality to the novel or the drama, as well as to poetry itself.[21]

Such a statement shows how close Cather's and Jewett's critical ideals had become. Both were more interested in character than in plot, both preferred emotional drama to drama of incident, both were concerned with the character of the locale, both used a spare, simple prose style.

It was Jewett's style for which Cather reserved her highest praise, an opinion echoed by Matthiessen in his study of Jewett. Style, Cather noted, is created by a "very personal quality of perception, a vivid and intensely personal experience of life." Of American authors, in addition to Jewett she cites only Hawthorne and Mark Twain as having achieved it. "Among fifty thousand books you will find very few writers who ever achieved a style at all." It is this "individual voice," Cather claims, that will make Jewett's works endure.[22]

Cather was not, however, the only writer whom Jewett influenced. Perhaps a dozen more should be named. Alice Brown (1857–1948), another local

colorist from Jewett's seacoast region, was a great
admirer. The two knew one another, they read each
other's works, and Brown settled permanently in the
Beacon Hill area of Boston near Annie Fields's
home.[23]

Kate Chopin (1851–1904) said that she knew no
better stories from which to study technique than
those of Sarah Orne Jewett.[24] Chopin had studied
"A White Heron" among others; it probably was the
model for her own story "Caline." Chopin's elliptical
prose style, as demonstrated in her great novel, *The
Awakening* (1899), undoubtedly reflects Jewett's
influence, as critics have suggested. It also anticipates Cather's mature style, especially that in *Death
Comes for the Archbishop*.[25]

Mary E. Wilkins Freeman (1852–1930), Jewett's
literary contemporary, also described New England
rural life but with a far bleaker point of view. The
two women were literary friends and admired one
another's work. Jewett found Freeman's "An Object
of Love" an exemplary short story, and Freeman
thought "A White Heron" better than anything she
had done herself.[26]

Mary Noailles Murfree (1850–1922), who used
the pseudonym "Charles Egbert Craddock" to write
stories and novels set in Tennessee, was another
whom Jewett influenced. Murfree called Jewett her
favorite author, and Jewett admired Murfree's
work.[27] Jewett also criticized manuscripts by Massachusetts poet and novelist Helen Hunt Jackson
(1830–1885), and Alice French (1850–1934), alias
"Octave Thanet," who wrote works set in the Middle
West. Others who wrote under Jewett's influence
include Dorothy Canfield Fisher (1879–1958),
Laura Richards (1850–1943), May Sinclair
(1865–1946), Ruth Suckow (1892–1960), Zona Gale
(1874–1938), and Mary Ellen Chase (1887–1973).

Even Truman Capote (b. 1924) has listed Jewett, along with Willa Cather, as one of his two favorite authors.[28]

One of the more interesting, if somewhat negative, influences Jewett had was on Edith Wharton (1862–1937). Wharton claimed that she had written in rebellion against the "rose-coloured" vision of her "predecessors," Freeman and Jewett. In her autobiography Wharton explained the motivation for her grim novel *Ethan Frome*.

For years I had wanted to draw life as it really was in the derelict mountain villages of New England, a life even in my time, and a thousand fold more a generation earlier, utterly unlike that seen through the rose-coloured spectacles of my predecessors, Mary Wilkins and Sarah Orne Jewett.[29]

Wharton's criticism is considerably off the mark. Indeed one suspects that she had not read much, if any, of Mary E. Wilkins Freeman, whose vision was anything but "rose-coloured." It is true, of course, that Jewett's characters have a positive, take-charge attitude toward life that is far different from the grim resignation and tragedy that dominate Wharton's world. But it is not fair to imply that Jewett's view is any less realistic or valuable than Wharton's; they are simply different. Edith Wharton did respect Jewett enough, however, to consider her her "predecessor" in the field and to make a pilgrimage by motorcar to Jewett's home in South Berwick in July 1905.[30] This was shortly before the publication of her first major novel, *The House of Mirth*.

Through her influence and through the continuing appeal of her works Sarah Orne Jewett has earned a permanent and important place in world literature. In 1929 F. O. Matthiessen judged her one of the two greatest American women writers, along with Emily Dickinson.[31] Today we would have to expand that list. But we must still agree with Willa Cather's 1913 tribute to Jewett in her dedication of *O Pioneers!* It reads: "To the memory of Sarah Orne Jewett in whose Beautiful and delicate work there is the perfection that endures."

Notes

1. TRANSFIGURATION THROUGH FRIENDSHIP: INTRODUCTION AND BIOGRAPHICAL SKETCH

All quotations in this chapter that are not documented are from Annie Adams Fields, ed., *Letters of Sarah Orne Jewett* (Boston: Houghton Mifflin Co., 1911), and Richard Cary, ed., *Sarah Orne Jewett Letters*, enl. and rev. (Waterville, Maine: Colby College Press, 1967).

1. Nina Baym, *Women's Fiction: A Guide to Novels by and about Women in America, 1820–1870* (Ithaca, N.Y.: Cornell University Press, 1978), p. 11.
2. Ann Douglas Wood, "The Literature of Impoverishment: The Women Local Colorists in America 1865–1914," *Women's Studies* 1 (1972):6, n. 12.
3. As cited in Susan Allen Toth, "Sarah Orne Jewett and Friends: A Community of Interest," *Studies in Short Fiction* 9, no. 3 (Summer 1972):235. My emphasis added.
4. Theodore Jewett Eastman, *A List of the Books from the Bequest of Theodore Jewett Eastman that Bear the Marks of Ownership of Sarah Orne Jewett* (Cambridge, Mass.: Harvard College Library, 1933), pp. 34–35.
5. Manuscript diary 1871–1879, Houghton MS. Am 1743.1 (341), Houghton Library, Harvard University. This and following manuscript materials are cited by permission of the Houghton Library, Harvard University.
6. Manuscript diary 1871–1879, entry for 3 May 1871.

7. Manuscript diary 1867–1868, Houghton bMS Am 1743.26 (3), entry for 29 September 1867, Houghton Library, Harvard University.

8. Manuscript diary 1871–1879, entry for 3 October 1872.

9. Manuscript diary 1869, Houghton bMS Am 1743.26 (4), entry for 30 January 1869, Houghton Library, Harvard University.

10. Barbara Welter, "The Cult of True Womanhood: 1820–1860," *American Quarterly* 18, no. 2, pt. 1 (Summer 1966):151–174.

11. Manuscript Diary 1869, entry for 2 September 1869.

12. Everett Carter, *Howells and the Age of Realism* (Hamden, Conn.: Archon Books, 1966), p. 20.

13. Carter, p. 118.

14. "A Bit of Shore Life," *Old Friends and New* (Boston: Houghton, Osgood, 1879), p. 263.

15. Helen Howe, *The Gentle Americans, 1864–1960, Biography of a Breed* (New York: Harper, 1965), pp. 83 ff.

16. Richard Cary, "The Other Face of Jewett's Coin," *American Literary Realism* 2, no. 3 (Fall 1969):264.

17. Social historians and sociologists have found this to be a common nineteenth-century relationship between women. See especially William R. Taylor and Christopher Lasch, "Two 'Kindred Spirits': Sorority and Family in New England, 1839–1846," *New England Quarterly* 36, no. 1 (March 1963):23–41; Carroll Smith-Rosenberg, "The Female World of Love and Ritual: Relations between Women in Nineteenth-Century America," *SIGNS* 1, no. 1 (Autumn 1975):1–29.

18. Rebecca West, "Introduction," *The Only Rose and Other Stories* (London: Jonathan Cape, 1937), p. 7.

19. A collection of Jewett's letters to Dresel are now in the Colby College Library and were published by Richard Cary, "Jewett to Dresel: 33 Letters," *Colby Library Quarterly*, 11, no. 1 (March 1975):13–49. There are 43 others in the Butler Library, Columbia University, and several more in the Alderman Library, University of Virginia. Most of the Violet Paget

correspondence is in the Colby College Library and was published in Cary, ed., *Sarah Orne Jewett Letters* (1967). The extensive Mary Rice Jewett collection is in the library of the Society for the Preservation of New England Antiquities in Boston; the Lily Munger letters are in the Alderman Library; the Dawes letters are in The Library of Congress and were printed in *Colby Library Quarterly* 8, no. 3 (Sept. 1968):97–138. The most important published collections are the Cary 1967 edition and the Fields 1911 volume.

20. Fields to Mrs. Charles Fairchild, 20 August 1909. Boston Public Library MS. 605. Cited by courtesy of the Trustees of the Boston Public Library.

2. THE ARTIST AS A YOUNG WOMAN: FROM *Play Days* TO *Deephaven* AND *Old Friends and New*

1. Manuscript diary 1871–1879, entry for 13 July 1872, Houghton Library, Harvard University.
2. Manuscript diary 1871–1879, entries for 17 July 1872, and n. d. 1874, respectively.
3. "On *Middlemarch*," unpublished manuscript, Houghton MS. Am 1743.22 (67), Houghton Library, Harvard University.
4. As cited in Glen L. Nagel and James Nagel, *Sarah Orne Jewett: A Reference Guide* (Boston: G. K. Hall & Co., 1978), p. 1.
5. *Atlantic Monthly* 39 (June 1877):759, as cited in Nagel, p. 2.
6. *Eclectic* 25 (June 1877):760, as cited in Nagel, p. 2.
7. *Good Company* 4 (3 November 1877):288, as cited in Nagel, p. 3.

3. CITY VERSUS COUNTRY: 1880–1886

1. Annie Adams Fields, ed., *Letters of Sarah Orne Jewett* (Boston: Houghton Mifflin Co., 1911), p. 20.

2. Richard Cary, ed., *Sarah Orne Jewett Letters* (Waterville, Maine: Colby College Press, 1967), p. 56.
3. Jean E. Kennard, *Victims of Convention* (Hamden, Conn.: Archon Books, 1978).
4. Kennard, chap. 2.
5. *The White Heron,* dir. Jane Morrison, Learning Corporation of America, 1978.
6. Annis Pratt, "Women and Nature in Modern Fiction," *Contemporary Literature* 13, no. 4 (Fall 1972):479.

4. ISOLATION VERSUS COMMUNITY: 1886–1895

1. Philip B. Eppard, " 'Dan's Wife': A Newly Discovered Sarah Orne Jewett Story," *Colby Library Quarterly* 12, no. 2 (June 1976):101–102.
2. Nina Auerbach, *Communities of Women: An Idea in Fiction* (Cambridge: Harvard University Press, 1978), p. 10.

5. *The Country of the Pointed Firs* AND OTHER LATE WORKS: 1896–1910

1. The publishing information is primarily from Clara Carter Weber and Carl J. Weber, *A Bibliography of the Published Writings of Sarah Orne Jewett* (Waterville, Maine: Colby College Press, 1949), p. 18. The details about the changes made between the magazine and the book text were provided by Richard Cary in "Jewett to Dresel: 33 Letters," *Colby Library Quarterly* 11, no. 1 (March 1975):45, n. 5.
2. John Eldridge Frost, *Sarah Orne Jewett* (Kittery Point, Maine: The Gundalow Club, 1960), p. 104.
3. Glen L. Nagel and James Nagel, *Sarah Orne Jewett: A Reference Guide* (Boston: G. K. Hall & Co., 1978), pp. 31–33.
4. These critics, all cited in Nagel and Nagel, include: Granville Hicks, p. 68; Howard Mumford Jones, p.

       81; Edward Wagenknecht, p. 92; Warner Berthoff,
       pp. 103–104; Hyatt Waggoner, pp. 105–106; Irving
       Howe, p. 138; Carlos Baker, p. 151.
   5. Warner Berthoff, *The Ferment of Realism: American
       Literature 1884–1919* (New York: The Free Press,
       1965), p. 99.
   6. David Bonnell Green, ed. *The World of Dunnet Land-
       ing, A Sarah Orne Jewett Collection* (Lincoln: Univer-
       sity of Nebraska Press, 1962).
   7. Rosamond Thaxter, *Sandpiper, The Life of Celia Thax-
       ter* (Sanbornville, New Hampshire: Wake-Brook
       House, 1962), p. 237. Subsequent references appear
       in the text.
   8. Lyman V. Rutledge, *The Isles of Shoals in Lore and
       Legend* (Barre, Mass.: Barre Publishers, 1965), p.
       100.
   9. See Josephine Donovan, "The Unpublished Love
       Poems of Sarah Orne Jewett," *Frontiers 4,* no. 3
       (January 1980):26–31.
  10. Ferman Bishop, "Henry James Criticizes *The Tory
       Lover,*" *American Literature* 27 (May 1955):264, as
       cited in Richard Cary, *Sarah Orne Jewett* (New York:
       Twayne, 1962), p. 152.

6. Criticism and Influence

   1. Richard Cary, ed., *Sarah Orne Jewett Letters,* enl. and
       rev. (Waterville, Maine: Colby College Press, 1967),
       pp. 118–121, 123–124, 125–129, 140–141.
   2. Annie Adams Fields, ed., *Letters of Sarah Orne Jewett,*
       (Boston: Houghton Mifflin Co., 1911), p. 47.
   3. Laura E. Richards, *Stepping Westward* (New York:
       Appleton, 1931), p. 369.
   4. Unless otherwise noted, all Jewett's advice to Cather
       is from Fields, ed., *Letters,* pp. 234–235, 245–250.
   5. Richard Cary, "Jewett on Writing Short Stories,"
       Colby Library Quarterly 6, no. 10 (June 1964):431.
   6. F. O. Matthiessen, *American Renaissance: Art and Ex-
       pression in the Age of Emerson and Whitman* (New York:
       Oxford University Press, 1941), pp. 602–603.

7. C. Carroll Hollis, "Letters of Sarah Orne Jewett to Anna Laurens Dawes," *Colby Library Quarterly* 8, no. 3 (September 1968):98.

8. Warner Berthoff, *The Ferment of Realism: American Literature 1884–1919* (New York: The Free Press, 1965), p. 291.

9. Alfred Kazin, *On Native Grounds* (New York: Reynal and Hitchcock, 1942), p. 18.

10. Fields, ed., *Letters*, pp. 72–73.

11. Unless otherwise noted, all Jewett's critical comments that follow are from Fields, ed., *Letters*, pp. 55–56, 77–79, 112, 196–197, 248.

12. This advice is cited variously by Cather herself. See her 1922 preface to *Alexander's Bridge* and also her essay "Miss Jewett," *Not under Forty* (New York: Knopf, 1936), p. 88.

13. As cited in Cather's 1925 preface to *The Best Short Stories of Sarah Orne Jewett.*

14. Cary, ed., *Sarah Orne Jewett Letters*, p. 52.

15. Robert E. Spiller et al., eds., *Literary History of the United States*, 3rd ed. rev., 3 vols. (New York: Macmillan, 1963), 1:845.

16. Cary, ed., *Sarah Orne Jewett Letters*, p. 51.

17. La Salle Corbell Pickett, *Across My Path, Memories of People I Have Known* (New York: Brentano's, 1916; rpt. 1970), p. 145.

18. Cary, ed., *Sarah Orne Jewett Letters*, p. 91.

19. *Ibid.*, p. 21.

20. "Willa Cather Talks of Work," *Philadelphia Record*, 9 August 1913, in Bernice Slote, ed., *The Kingdom of Art: Willa Cather's First Principles and Critical Statements 1893–1896* (Lincoln: University of Nebraska Press, 1966), pp. 446–449.

21. Cather, *Not Under Forty*, p. 50.

22. *Ibid.*, p. 95.

23. Dorothea Walker, *Alice Brown* (New York: Twayne, 1974), p. 30; Susan Allen Toth, "Sarah Orne Jewett and Friends: A Community of Interest," *Studies in Short Fiction* 9, no. 3 (Summer 1972):238–241.

24. Per Seyersted, *Kate Chopin: A Critical Biography*

(Baton Rouge: Louisiana State University Press, 1969), pp. 52, 121, 195.

25.   These points are made by Lewis Leary, Introduction to *The Awakening and Other Stories* (New York: Holt, Rinehart and Winston, 1970), pp. x, xv. If Chopin influenced Cather, it is ironic, as Cather had written a negative review of *The Awakening* when it appeared. See William M. Curtin, ed., *The World and the Parish, Willa Cather's Articles and Reviews 1893–1902*, 2 vols (Lincoln: University of Nebraska Press, 1970), 1:697–699.

26.   F. O. Matthiessen, *Sarah Orne Jewett* (Boston: Houghton Mifflin Co., 1929), p. 84; Toth, "Sarah Orne Jewett and Friends," pp. 236–238.

27.   Edd Winfield Park, *Charles Egbert Craddock (Mary Noailles Murfree)* (Chapel Hill: University of North Carolina Press, 1941), pp. 96, 127–128, 150.

28.   Anne Taylor Fleming, "The Private World of Truman Capote," *New York Times Magazine,* 9 July 1978, p. 24. Capote also listed Jewett as a major influence in his 1968 preface to *Other Voices, Other Rooms* (New York: Random House, 1968), p. x.

29.   Edith Wharton, *A Backward Glance* (New York: Scribner's, 1933; rpt. 1962), p. 293.

30.   R. W. B. Lewis, *Edith Wharton: A Biography* (New York: Harper, 1965), p. 150.

31.   Matthiessen, *Sarah Orne Jewett,* p. 152.

Bibliography

I. Works by Sarah Orne Jewett

Deephaven. Boston: James R. Osgood and Company, 1877. Contents: "Kate Lancaster's Plan," "The Brandon House and the Lighthouse," "My Lady Brandon and the Widow Jim," "Deephaven Society," "The Captains," "Danny," "Captain Sands," "The Circus at Denby," "Cunner-Fishing," "Mrs. Bonny," "In Shadow," "Miss Chauncey," "Last Days in Deephaven."

Play Days, A Book of Stories For Children. Boston: Houghton, Osgood and Company, 1878. Contents: "Discontent," "The Water Dolly," "Prissy's Visit," "My Friend the Housekeeper," "Marigold House," "Nancy's Doll," "The Best China Saucer," "The Desert Islanders," "Half-Done Polly," "Woodchucks," "The Kitten's Ghost," "The Pepper-Owl," "The Shipwrecked Buttons," "The Yellow Kitten," "Patty's Dull Christmas," "Beyond the Toll-Gate."

Old Friends and New. Boston: Houghton, Osgood and Company, 1879. Contents: "A Lost Lover," "A Sorrowful Guest," "A Late Supper," "Mr. Bruce," "Miss Sydney's Flowers," "Lady Ferry," "A Bit of Shore Life."

Country By-Ways. Boston: Houghton, Mifflin and Company, 1881. Contents: "River Driftwood," "Andrew's Fortune," "An October Ride," "From a Mournful Villager," "An Autumn Holiday," "A Winter Drive," "Good Luck: A Girl's Story," "Miss Becky's Pilgrimage."

Betty Leicester's English Xmas, A New Chapter of An Old Story.
New York: Dodd, Mead & Co., 1894.

The Life of Nancy. Boston and New York: Houghton,
Mifflin and Company, 1895. Contents: "The Life of
Nancy," "Fame's Little Day," "A War Debt," "The
Hiltons' Holiday," "The Only Rose," "A Second
Spring," "Little French Mary," "The Guests of Mrs.
Timms," "A Neighbor's Landmark," "All My Sad
Captains."

The Country of the Pointed Firs. Boston and New York:
Houghton, Mifflin and Company, 1896.

The Queen's Twin and Other Stories. Boston and New York:
Houghton, Mifflin and Company, 1899. Contents:
"The Queen's Twin," "A Dunnet Shepherdess,"
"Where's Nora?" "Bold Words at the Bridge,"
"Martha's Lady," "The Coon Dog," "Aunt Cynthy
Dallett," "The Night Before Thanksgiving."

The Tory Lover. Boston and New York: Houghton, Mifflin
and Company, 1901.

An Empty Purse, A Christmas Story. Boston: The Merrymount Press, 1905.

Works Published Posthumously

Verses. Boston: The Merrymount Press, 1916.

The Uncollected Short Stories of Sarah Orne Jewett. Ed. with
intro. by Richard Cary. Waterville, Maine: Colby Col-
lege Press. 1971. Contents: "Jenny Garrow's Lovers,"
"The Girl with the Cannon Dresses," "The Orchard's
Grandmother," "Paper Roses," "Stolen Pleasures,"
"Hallowell's Pretty Sister," "A Guest at Home," "A
Dark Carpet," "The Hare and the Tortoise," "Miss
Manning's Minister," "The Becket Girls' Tree," "A
Visit Next Door," "A Garden Story," "A Christmas
Guest," "The Growtown 'Bugle,'" "The New
Methuselah," "Miss Parkins's Christmas Eve," "A Fi-
nancial Failure: The Story of A New England Woo-
ing," "A Way Station," "Peg's Little Chair," "An
Every-Day Girl," "Peach-tree Joe," "Told in the
Tavern," "In a Country Practice," "A Dark Night,"
"An Empty Purse," "A Change of Heart," "A Village
Patriot," "A Pinch of Salt," "The First Sunday in

June," "The Gray Mills of Farley," "The Parshley
Celebration," "A Landlocked Sailor," "The Stage
Tavern," "The Foreigner," "Elleneen," "The Green
Bonnet: A Story of Easter Day," "A Born Farmer,"
"The Green Bowl," "The Honey Tree," "The Spur of
the Moment," "Sister Peacham's Turn," "The Lost
Turkey," "A Spring Sunday."

Letters

The Letters of Sarah Orne Jewett. Edited by Annie Fields.
Boston and New York: Houghton, Mifflin Company,
1911.

Sarah Orne Jewett Letters. Enl. and rev. Edited by Richard
Cary. Waterville, Maine: Colby College Press, 1967.

Cary, Richard. "Jewett to Dresel: 33 Letters." *Colby Library
Quarterly* 11 (March 1975):13–49.

Hollis, C. Carroll. "Letters of Sarah Orne Jewett to Anna
Laurens Dawes." *Colby Library Quarterly* 8 (September
1968):97–138.

Lucey, William L., S. J. " 'We New Englanders . . .': Let-
ters of Sarah Orne Jewett to Louise Imogen Guiney."
*Records of the American Catholic Historical Society of
Philadelphia* 70 (1959):58–64.

II. SELECTED WORKS ABOUT SARAH ORNE JEWETT

Biographical Sources

Cather, Willa. "148 Charles Street" and "Miss Jewett." In
Not Under Forty. New York: Knopf, 1953, pp. 52–95.

Frost, John Eldridge. *Sarah Orne Jewett.* Kittery Point,
Maine: The Gundalow Club, 1960.

Harkins, E. F., and Johnston, C. H. L. *Little Pilgrimages
Among the Women Who Have Written Famous Books.*
Boston: Page, 1902, pp. 43–58.

Howe, Helen. *The Gentle Americans 1864–1960: Biography
of a Breed.* New York: Harper & Row, 1965.

Howe, Mark A. DeWolfe. *Memories of a Hostess: A Chronicle of Eminent Friendships Drawn Chiefly from the Diaries of Mrs. James T. Fields.* Boston: Atlantic Monthly Press, 1922.

James, Henry. "Mr. and Mrs. James T. Fields." *Atlantic Monthly* 116 (July 1915):21–31.

Matthiessen, Francis Otto. *Sarah Orne Jewett.* Boston and New York: Houghton Mifflin Company, 1929.

Pickett, LaSalle Corbell. *Across My Path: Memories of People I Have Known.* New York: Brentano's, 1916.

Richards, Laura. *Stepping Westward.* New York: Appleton, 1931.

Spofford, Harriet Prescott. *A Little Book of Friends.* Boston: Little, Brown, 1916.

Winslow, Helen M. *Literary Boston of To-Day.* Boston: Page, 1902.

Bibliographies

Cary, Richard. "Some Bibliographic Ghosts of Sarah Orne Jewett." *Colby Library Quarterly* 8 (September 1968):139–145.

Eichelberger, Clayton L., comp. "Sarah Orne Jewett (1849–1909): A Critical Bibliography of Secondary Comment." *American Literary Realism* 2 (Fall 1969):189–262.

Nagel, Gwen L. and Nagel, James, comps. *Sarah Orne Jewett: A Reference Guide.* Boston: G. K. Hall & Company, 1978.

Weber, Clara Carter, and Weber, Carl J., comps. *A Bibliography of the Published Writings of Sarah Orne Jewett.* Waterville, Maine: Colby College Press, 1949.

III.   CRITICISM

Books

Auchincloss, Louis. *Pioneers and Caretakers: A Study of 9 American Women Novelists.* Minneapolis: University of Minnesota Press, 1965.

Buchan, A. M. *"Our Dear Sarah": An Essay on Sarah Orne Jewett.* Washington University Studies, No. 24. St. Louis: Washington University Press, 1953. Reprinted in Cary, Richard, *Appreciation of Sarah Orne Jewett.*

Cary, Richard. *Sarah Orne Jewett.* Twayne United States Authors Series, No. 19. New York: Twayne, 1962.

Cary, Richard, ed. *Appreciation of Sarah Orne Jewett: 29 Interpretive Essays.* Waterville, Maine: Colby College Press, 1973.

Eastman, Theodore Jewett. *A Lits of the Books from the Bequest of Theodore Jewett Eastman That Bear the Marks of Ownership of Sarah Orne Jewett.* Cambridge: Harvard College Library, 1933.

Sougnac, Jean. *Sarah Orne Jewett.* Paris: Jouve et Cie., 1937.

Thorp, Margaret F. *Sarah Orne Jewett.* University of Minnesota Pamphlets on American Writers, No. 61. Minneapolis: University of Minnesota Press, 1966.

Westbrook, Perry D. *Acres of Flint: Writers of Rural New England 1870–1900.* Washington, D. C.: Scarecrow Press, 1951.

Articles

Blanc, Marie Thérèse ("Th. Bentzon"). "Le Roman de la femme-médicin." *Revue des Deux Mondes* 67 (1 February 1885):598–632. Translation reprinted in Cary, Richard, *Appreciation of Sarah Orne Jewett.*

Berthoff, Warner. "The Art of Jewett's *Pointed Firs.*" *New England Quarterly* 32 (March 1959):31–53. Reprinted in Cary, Richard *Appreciation of Sarah Orne Jewett,* and Green, David Bonnell, *The World of Dunnet Landing.*

Bishop, Ferman. "Henry James Criticizes *The Tory Lover.*" *American Literature* 27 (May 1955):262–264. Reprinted in Cary, Richard, *Appreciation of Sarah Orne Jewett.*

Cary, Richard. "Jewett on Writing Short Stories." *Colby Library Quarterly* 6 (June 1964):425–440.

Cary, Richard. "Jewett's Literary Canons." *Colby Library Quarterly* 7 (June 1965):82–87.

Cary, Richard. "Introduction" to Sarah Orne Jewett,

Deephaven and Other Stories. New Haven: College and University Press, 1966, pp. 7–23.

Cary, Richard. "Miss Jewett and Madame Blanc." *Colby Library Quarterly* 7 (September 1967):467–488.

Cary, Richard. "Sarah Orne Jewett (1849–1909)." *American Literary Realism* 1 (Fall 1967):61–66.

Cary, Richard. "The Other Face of Jewett's Coin." *American Literary Realism* 2 (Fall 1969):263–270.

Cary, Richard. "Violet Paget to Sarah Orne Jewett." *Colby Library Quarterly* 9 (December 1970):235–243.

Cary, Richard. "The Uncollected Short Stories of Sarah Orne Jewett." *Colby Library Quarterly* 9 (December 1971):385–408. Reprinted in Cary, Richard, *The Uncollected Short Stories of Sarah Orne Jewett* and *Appreciation of Sarah Orne Jewett*.

Cather, Willa. "Preface" to *The Best Short Stories of Sarah Orne Jewett*. 2 vols. Boston: Houghton Mifflin Company, 1925, 1:ix–xix.

Donovan, Josephine. "A Woman's Vision of Transcendence: A New Interpretation of the Works of Sarah Orne Jewett." *Massachusetts Review* 21, no. 2 (Summer 1980).

Donovan, Josephine. "The Unpublished Love Poetry of Sarah Orne Jewett." *Frontiers, A Journal of Women Studies* 4, no. 3 (January 1980):26–31.

Donovan, Josephine. "Sarah Orne Jewett," in *Guide to American Women Writers, A Critical Reference Guide from Colonial Times to the Present*. Edited by Lina Mainiero. Vol. 2. New York: Frederick Ungar, 1979.

Fike, Francis. "An Interpretation of *Pointed Firs*." *New England Quarterly* 34 (December 1961):478–491. Reprinted in Cary, Richard, *Appreciation of Sarah Orne Jewett*.

Forrey, Carolyn. "The New Woman Revisited." *Women's Studies* 2 (1974):37–56.

Garnett, Edward. "Books Too Little Known: Miss Sarah Orne Jewett's Tales." *Academy and Literature* 65 (11 July 1903):40–41. Reprinted in Cary, Richard, *Appreciation of Sarah Orne Jewett*.

Green, David Bonnell. "The World of Dunnet Landing." *New England Quarterly* 34 (December 1961):514–517.

Reprinted in Green, David Bonnell, *The World of Dunnet Landing*.

Green, David Bonnell. ed. *The World of Dunnet Landing, A Sarah Orne Jewett Collection*. Lincoln: University of Nebraska Press, 1962.

Hobbs, Glenda. "Pure and Passionate: Female Friendship in Sarah Orne Jewett's 'Martha's Lady.' " *Studies in Short Fiction* (forthcoming).

Jobes, Katherine T. "From Stowe's Eagle Island to Jewett's 'A White Heron.' " *Colby Library Quarterly* 10 (December 1974):515–521.

Levy, Babette May. "Mutations in New England Local Color." *New England Quarterly* 19 (September 1946):338–358. Reprinted in Cary, Richard, *Appreciation of Sarah Orne Jewett*.

Magowan, Robin. "Pastoral and the Art of Landscape in *The Country of the Pointed Firs.*" *New England Quarterly* 36 (June 1963):229–240. Reprinted in Cary, Richard, *Appreciation of Sarah Orne Jewett*.

Magowan, Robin. "Fromentin and Jewett: Pastoral Narrative in the Nineteenth Century." *Comparative Literature* 16 (Fall 1964):331–337.

More, Paul Elmer. "A Writer of New England." *Nation* 91 (27 October 1910):386–387. Reprinted in Cary, Richard, *Appreciation of Sarah Orne Jewett*.

Morgan, Ellen. "The Atypical Woman: Nan Prince in the Literary Transition to Feminism." *The Kate Chopin Newletter* 2 (Fall 1976):33–37.

Pratt, Annis. "Women and Nature in Modern Fiction." *Contemporary Literature* 13 (Fall 1972):476–490.

Rhode, Robert D. "Sarah Orne Jewett and 'The Palpable Present Intimate.' " *Colby Library Quarterly* 8 (September 1968):146–155. Reprinted in Cary, Richard, *Appreciation of Sarah Orne Jewett*.

Shackford, Martha Hale. "Sarah Orne Jewett." *Sewanee Review* 30 (January 1922):20–26. Reprinted in Cary, Richard, *Appreciation of Sarah Orne Jewett* and Green, David Bonnell, *The World of Dunnet Landing*.

Short, Clarice. "Studies in Gentleness." *Western Humanities Review* 11 (Autumn 1957):387–393. Reprinted in Cary, Richard, *Appreciation of Sarah Orne Jewett.*

Smith, Eleanor M. "The Literary Relationship of Sarah Orne Jewett and Willa Sibert Cather." *New England Quarterly* 29 (December 1956):472–492. Reprinted in Cary, Richard, *Appreciation of Sarah Orne Jewett.*

Stevenson, Catherine Barnes. "The Double Consciousness of the Narrator in Sarah Orne Jewett's Fiction." *Colby Library Quarterly* 11 (March 1975):1–12.

Thompson, Charles Miner. "The Art of Miss Jewett." *Atlantic Monthly* 94 (October 1904):485–497. Reprinted in Cary, Richard, *Appreciation of Sarah Orne Jewett.*

Toth, Susan Allen. "Sarah Orne Jewett and Friends: A Community of Interest." *Studies in Short Fiction* 9 (Summer 1972):233–241.

Tutweiler, Julia R. "Two New England Writers in Relation to Their Art and to Each Other." *Gunton's Magazine* 25 (November 1903):419–425. Reprinted in Cary, Richard, *Appreciation of Sarah Orne Jewett.*

Waggoner, Hyatt H. "The Unity of *The Country of the Pointed Firs.*" *Twentieth-Century Literature* 5 (July 1959):67–73. Reprinted in Cary, Richard, *Appreciation of Sarah Orne Jewett* and Green, David Bonnell, *The World of Dunnet Landing.*

Weber, Carl J. "New England Through French Eyes Fifty Years Ago." *New England Quarterly* 20 (September 1947):385–396.

West, Rebecca. Introduction to *The Only Rose and Other Stories.* London: Jonathan Cape, 1937, pp. 7–14.

Wood, Ann Douglas. "The Literature of Impoverishment: The Women Local Colorists in America 1865–1914." *Women's Studies* 1 (1972):3–46.

Index

In the same series (continued from page ii)